T0163354

MISSOURI
AT SEA

PROJECT SPONSORS

Missouri Center for the Book

**Western Historical Manuscript Collection,
University of Missouri—Columbia**

MISSOURI HERITAGE READERS
General Editor, Rebecca B. Schroeder

Each Missouri Heritage Reader explores a particular aspect of the state's rich cultural heritage. Focusing on people, places, historical events, and the details of daily life, these books illustrate the ways in which people from all parts of the world contributed to the development of the state and the region. The books incorporate documentary and oral history, folklore, and informal literature in a way that makes these resources accessible to all Missourians.

Intended primarily for adult new readers, these books will also be invaluable to readers of all ages interested in the cultural and social history of Missouri.

BOOKS IN THE SERIES

MISSOURI AT SEA

WARSHIPS WITH
SHOW-ME STATE NAMES

Richard E. Schroeder

UNIVERSITY OF MISSOURI PRESS
COLUMBIA

Library of Congress Cataloging-in-Publication Data
Schroeder, Richard E.
Missouri at sea : warships with Show-Me State names /
Richard E. Schroeder
p. cm. — (Missouri heritage readers)
Includes index.
ISBN 978-0-8262-1523-9 (alk. paper)
1. Missouri (Battleship : BB 63) 2. Warships—United States. 3.
Warships—Confederate States of America. 4. Missouri—History,
Naval. I. Title. II. Series.
VA65.M59S37 2004
359.8'3'0973—dc22
2003027386

∞™ This paper meets the requirements of the
American National Standard for Permanence of Paper
for Printed Library Materials, Z39.48, 1984.

Typefaces: Gill Sans and Palatino

Contents

Contents

Foreword

In July of 1918, my father, also named Ike Skelton, dropped out of high school in his hometown of Higginsville, Missouri, misrepresented his age, and joined the U.S. Navy. He was assigned to be a fireman on the battleship named for his home state—the *Missouri*, flagship of the Second Division of the Atlantic Fleet. He was discharged from active duty in 1919.

Although my father returned to high school and received both bachelor's and law degrees from the University of Missouri, his service in the navy was a defining event in his life. He was immensely proud of his service and mandated that the only thing that should appear on his grave marker, other than his name and dates of birth and death, was the following: U.S. Navy, World War I.

In a sense, my father's naval service was a defining event in my life, also. He spoke to me often of his training at Great Lakes, and of his life on board the *Missouri*. He inspired my lifelong interest in the navy, and in military history in general, which I carried with me during my own studies at the University of Missouri, and which has proved invaluable to me in my work as ranking Democrat on the House Armed Services Committee.

Rick Schroeder's book will make a valuable contribution to Missouri and U.S. history and will remind Missourians of the contribution their citizens, and the ships named for their state, have made to American history and national security. It will tell not only the story of Missouri warships like the *Missouri* my father served on, and its more famous successor *Missouri* from World War II, but also the story of heroic Missouri sailors, including some awarded the Medal of Honor.

As the son of a proud navy veteran from Missouri, and as a graduate of the University of Missouri with a degree in history, I welcome this book.

Ike Skelton
Member of Congress

Acknowledgments

This book is dedicated to my wife, Leah, who patiently allowed me to "borrow" her kitchen counter on which most of this book was written. It is also dedicated to my mother, Rebecca Boies Schroeder, general editor of this series, who has inspired me with her love, energy, and sense of public service.

I also want to particularly thank my federal government colleagues in the National Archives and Records Administration, Navy and Marine Corps History Centers, and Department of Defense Visual Information Center, who generously helped my research and led me to the wonderful images used to enliven this text, and my fellow professors at National Defense University's Industrial College of the Armed Forces who read and critiqued the text. Finally, my thanks to my U.S. Army colleague Lieutenant Colonel Steve Oluic, who created the maps for this book. Any remaining errors are of course my own.

MISSOURI
AT SEA

Introduction

On August 26, 1843, the *Missouri*, the U.S. Navy's most modern warship, was en route to China carrying Caleb Cushing, who had been sent by President John Tyler to negotiate America's first commercial treaty with the Chinese. While stopped at the Rock of Gibraltar, the frigate caught fire and burned despite the best efforts of her crew and sailors of the British Royal Navy to save her.

Over one hundred years later, on September 2, 1945, representatives of the Japanese Empire climbed aboard the most modern and powerful battleship in the U.S. Navy—another *Missouri*—to surrender unconditionally to the Allies at the end of World War II.

In June 1998, *Missouri* returned to Pearl Harbor, Hawaii, to become a historic monument, and one month later, the newest and most powerful aircraft carrier in the world—*Harry S. Truman*—joined the navy.

Although the state of Missouri is hundreds of miles from an ocean, ships with Missouri names and connections have served the United States since the earliest days of Missouri statehood. Six years after Missouri joined the Union in 1821, work began in the Washington Navy Yard on a sloop of war that would be christened *St. Louis*, and in all, six ships have been named for the "Gateway City," including a cruiser that survived the Japanese attack on Pearl Harbor on December 7, 1941, and, with her great sister *Missouri*, helped defeat the Japanese in the Pacific Ocean. The first

Missouri was the first oceangoing steam frigate in the U.S. Navy, and the fourth, and last, *Missouri* was also the last— and most famous—American battleship of them all. As technological advances changed naval warfare, nuclear submarines began to patrol the seas. One was christened *Jefferson City*; another was named for one of Missouri's legendary sons, *Daniel Boone.* At the end of the twentieth century, a nuclear aircraft carrier named for President Harry S. Truman carried a crew of five thousand, and in the Middle East, a ship named for a young Missouri hero, *Cole,* was struck by anti-American terrorists.

From sailing ships, to Civil War ironclads, to the most powerful battleships, submarines, and aircraft carriers of the modern navy, over a century and a half of American naval history can be told through the story of vessels carrying names of Missouri heroes and Missouri places. This is the history of these ships and of their diplomatic and military service to the United States.

CHAPTER ONE

The Birth of the United States Navy

The First Warships with Missouri Names—
St. Louis and *Missouri*

In 1781, General George Washington wrote to his friend the French Count Lafayette: "It follows . . . as certain as night succeeds the day, that without a decisive naval force we can do nothing definitive—and with it everything honorable and glorious."

Many Americans, including Washington himself, were skilled, experienced soldiers who had fought alongside the British and felt confident against them. But by the time of the Revolution, Britain had perfected sail-powered wooden ships. The powerful British navy had fleets of battleships along with smaller, faster frigates and sloops that served as scouts and also acted as cruisers, protecting British commerce and attacking enemy vessels. The rebels could not hope to build a navy able to compete. They could, however, adopt guerrilla tactics to harass and plague their powerful enemy. Americans built or hired small, fast warships and put in command aggressive sailors such as John Paul Jones to attack British merchant ships. In 1778 America also sent Ben Franklin to negotiate a treaty with England's bitter rival, France, and it was a French fleet that supported General Washington and allowed him to cut off and capture a British army at Yorktown, Virginia, in 1781

3

and win American independence.

Even as Americans began to enjoy their new freedom they discovered the costs and burdens of liberty. Americans were suspicious of professional warriors and reluctant to pay to maintain a permanent navy, but they did want to trade with the whole world. Thomas Jefferson defined the role of the U.S. Navy for the next hundred years by arguing for a small number of modest warships to protect American commercial rights, and discourage powerful European enemies by threatening their own merchant ships. He believed the new United States was too weak to challenge the great European powers and should seek peaceful cooperation rather than confrontation. Not until the early twentieth century would the United States build a navy to match those of the leading world powers.

Still, the United States quickly became a trading powerhouse, with booming seaports. By 1820 only England had more trade with China than the United States, and the U.S. Navy had frigates and smaller warships all over the world whose captains made commercial treaties with local rulers, cooperated with the British navy, and acted as "policemen" to protect American rights, lives, and property.

In 1827, six years after Missouri joined the Union, the navy began building a twenty-gun sloop of war at the Washington Navy Yard. Measuring 127 feet long, weighing 700 tons, carrying a crew of 125 officers and men, and costing $125,000, this modest ship was perfectly suited to the duties of the American navy and to the modest role America then played in the world. One of eleven "sister ships" and named *St. Louis*, she was to serve all over the world and even to play the central role in a celebrated diplomatic crisis with a European empire.

Driven by the wind, the sloop could cruise for months at a time, stopping only for water and food for her crew. Two years after work had begun on her, *St. Louis* sailed under Commander John D. Sloat, leaving the naval base at

Hampton Roads on Chesapeake Bay February 1829 on her way to join the U.S. Navy's Pacific Squadron. She sailed around stormy Cape Horn at the southern tip of South America, arriving in Peru in June.

St. Louis patrolled the Pacific coast of South America for the next two years as Spanish colonies struggled to gain independence. American sailors were often caught between Latin American revolutionaries and Spanish authorities, with both sides sending out raiding ships, declaring blockades, and harassing neutral merchants and sailors. *St. Louis* escorted American merchant ships; her captain interceded with local officials on behalf of Americans; and her crew guarded the cash earned by American merchants. In spite of America's natural sympathy for the "Great Liberator," Simón Bolívar, and other revolutionary heroes fighting European domination, the navy tried to remain neutral unless American citizens were threatened. Unfortunately, Commander Sloat soon found himself and *St. Louis* caught up in Peruvian politics. Before today's instant, worldwide communication, American naval officers often had to rely on their common sense, the force of their guns, and vague written instructions laying out American foreign policy.

In the spring of 1831, Peruvian President Augustín Gamarra thought that his "notoriously unreliable" vice president, one General La Fuente, was planning to overthrow him and sent soldiers to his house to kill him. La Fuente's wife held the soldiers at bay while he fled in his nightshirt. At five in the morning he arrived by canoe at the *St. Louis.* Commander Sloat gave him "asylum against the mob," and the commodore of the Pacific Squadron wrote the American diplomatic representative in the Peruvian capital, Lima, praising Sloat's conduct as "honorable, benevolent, and discreet."

Commander Sloat then found himself stuck with the "unreliable" general for almost a month and was forced to ask the secretary of the navy to reimburse him for almost one thousand dollars "spent on entertaining" his guest. Because the navy had no funds for such activities, President Andrew Jackson had to ask Congress to appropriate the money.

St. Louis next sailed to Pensacola, Florida, in October 1832, under Commander John T. Newton. Ten years later, Newton, by then a captain, would command the first Missouri as she steamed across the Atlantic carrying U.S. Commissioner to China Caleb Cushing. Newton and St. Louis joined the West Indies Squadron, and until 1838 the ship patrolled the Caribbean, encouraging trade, suppressing piracy and the slave trade, and protecting American commercial rights.

After repairs at the Brooklyn Navy Yard, St. Louis again sailed in June 1839 to join the Pacific Squadron off California, becoming the first U.S. Navy ship to visit the port of San Francisco in Mexican California. While off California, St. Louis became involved in tensions between Mexican governors and American and British settlers. The number of settlers was growing, and fearing that they were plotting to overthrow him, California governor Juan Bautista Alvarado ordered forty-eight Americans and Britons arrested. After protests by St. Louis's commander, French Forrest, and the British consul, Alvarado set the prisoners free.

By the spring of 1843, St. Louis had returned to the East Coast. She was dispatched from Norfolk, Virginia, to join the East Indies Squadron. On that trip, she sailed around the Cape of Good Hope at the southern tip of Africa and through the Indian Ocean. China and the Indonesian Islands were rich sources of trade for Europeans and Americans, and St. Louis was part of the force sent to suppress Indonesian piracy and assure that American merchants received their share of the Chinese market.

In the 1830s the British had dominated trade with the

decaying Chinese empire. By 1842 the U.S. Navy was pursuing American commercial interests, and Captain Lawrence Kearny was visiting Chinese ports, seeking treaties to allow American merchants and ships the same rights enjoyed by the British. To finish the work begun by Kearny, the United States decided to send a representative to negotiate a formal treaty with China. To transport this minister, Caleb Cushing, the navy chose its most modern ship, the steam frigate *Missouri*.

The navy's first two oceangoing steam frigates were named for America's great rivers: the Mississippi and the Missouri. American and European inventors had been experimenting with steam power for decades, but early steamships were not very practical for war because their giant side paddle wheels limited the number of guns they could carry. The fragile paddle wheels were also vulnerable to enemy fire, and on long voyages, the engines burned more coal than the ships could carry. A steamer with its paddle wheels shot to pieces was worse off than an old-fashioned sailing ship, and steam only showed its clear advantages over sail once practical underwater screw propellers were invented. By the time Congress directed the navy to build the two "sea steamers" in March 1839, the British and French navies already had over a dozen steamers each in their fleets. *Missouri* and *Mississippi* were the first American warships in which machinery and coal successfully replaced the sails and wind that had moved ships for thousands of years.

The sister ships were built under the active supervision of one of the navy's finest officers, Matthew Calbraith Perry, brother of Oliver Hazard Perry, the hero of the Battle of Lake Erie in the War of 1812. In 1853, Matthew Perry would lead the first expedition to open Japan to American trade, using *Mississippi* as his flagship. When launched at the New York Navy Yard in 1841, the ships were the largest in the U.S. Navy—each was 229 feet long, weighed 1,700

The first *Missouri* at sea. (Naval Historical Center)

tons, and carried crews of 226 men. Each had cost $570,000 and was armed with 10 guns. Still, aside from their engines, paddle wheels, and smokestacks, they were traditional wooden ships with masts and sails and would not have seemed out of place in the Revolutionary War. The navy was very pleased with the performance of the new ships, although the one test between them, a race from New York up the Potomac to the Washington Navy Yard in the spring of 1842, ended with *Missouri* running aground at Port Tobacco, Maryland, just south of Washington, on April 1, and the engines of *Mississippi* overheating. The ships consumed huge amounts of coal, but they had been designed to carry enough fuel to steam for twenty days.

In early 1842, *Missouri* conducted trials out of Washington, and the proud navy showed off its advanced new ship to thousands of visitors. After a cruise to the Gulf of

Mexico, she returned to Washington to take aboard Commissioner Cushing for his trip to China. Cushing carried his large library of books on diplomacy and China, letters from President John Tyler to the emperor of China, and instructions from Secretary of State Daniel Webster that "a leading object of the mission. . . is to secure the entry of the American ships into [Chinese] ports on terms as favorable as those [of] British merchants." He also packed a fine uniform: a blue coat with gilt buttons, white pantaloons with a gold stripe, and a "chapeau with a white plume." On August 6, 1843, President Tyler visited *Missouri* and watched the crew in action as the two huge paddle wheels smoothly propelled the ships "with noiseless accuracy" around Hampton Roads near Norfolk, Virginia. *Missouri* then left for Europe, carrying Cushing on his way to China. During sea trials and contests with her sister, *Mississippi*, *Missouri* had shown that her engines could drive her as fast as sixteen miles per hour, and in the next twelve days she proved she could steam across the Atlantic, her engines pushing her almost nonstop day and night.

Missouri arrived at the British naval base of Gibraltar, at the mouth of the Mediterranean Sea, on August 25 and saluted the British fortress and warships anchored under the famous Rock of Gibraltar. The next day, as the crew began loading coal and water and overhauling the steam engines, Captain John Newton and Commissioner Cushing went ashore to greet the American consul and British governor Sir Robert T. Wilson. That evening Captain Newton's visit was interrupted by word of fire aboard *Missouri*, and he rushed back with Governor Wilson and British Admiral Sir George Sartorius of the British battleship *Malabar* to try to save his ship. As Newton wrote in his report to the navy, he found "flames raging with violence, and the officers and crew exerting themselves to their utmost to overcome them." Despite the best efforts of the American crew and British sailors from *Malabar* and from Gibraltar, pumps and water buckets were no match for the fire, which was fanned by high winds. Newton flooded *Missouri*'s gunpowder magazines to prevent explosion; then, just before midnight, he abandoned ship, escaping down a rope to a waiting boat. At three in the morning the guns and magazine exploded, and the ship settled to the shallow bottom of the harbor.

Over a hundred years later, as another *Missouri* steamed toward Gibraltar in March 1946, the American consul at Gibraltar, C. Paul Fletcher, wrote a letter to Secretary of State James Byrnes in which he described a picture on the consulate wall showing "the falling of the [*Missouri*'s] mainmast, and explosion of the last gun, which occurred at the same moment. . . . On the spanker-boom is an unfortunate Bear which perished in the flames."

Aside from the "unfortunate Bear," a pet, Cushing lost his books and grand uniform, and the crew lost everything but the clothes they were wearing. While the battleship *Malabar* took in his crew, Newton had the unhappy task of reporting the loss of his ship to the navy. In his report on "the destruction of our noble ship," Newton said that despite "the sad and melancholy scene, I am happy to bear testimony to the zeal and firmness of all the officers [who were] honorable to themselves and to the service. The crew also did their duty like men, and deserve well of their country."

Included in his report is the testimony of three crewmen. One "coal heaver," John Sutton, went to a storeroom to get a scale to weigh coal. As he pulled the scale off a shelf, a wrench fell, too, breaking a glass container of turpentine. Sailors William J. Williams and Alfred Clam were working on the engine, and Clam's lamp ignited the dripping turpentine. They were unable to stop the fire before the flames reached the wooden hull and doomed the ship.

The U.S. Navy was not to have another *Missouri* for sixty years, but *Mississippi* had a long and distinguished career,

The first *Missouri* in flames at Gibraltar. (Naval Historical Center)

serving in the Mexican War and in the Civil War, both as part of the Union blockade and as one of the biggest and most powerful ships in Admiral David Farragut's fleet that attacked and captured New Orleans. While she had been built for ocean sailing, she spent her last days on the river for which she was named.

Less than two years after the British had come to the aid of the burning *Missouri* at Gibraltar, the sailors of *St. Louis* were able to help endangered British citizens in New Zealand. As *St. Louis* was returning to Norfolk from her China service, she stopped in March 1845 at the small British settlement of Russell in New Zealand. Commander Isaac McKeever learned that a native Maori chief, Honi Heke, was threatening to attack the settlement because of British violations of treaties and broken promises to respect Maori lands. Because the British had only a few soldiers and one small warship to defend the settlers, Commander McKeever met with Honi Heke and received his "pledge of safety to the innocent women and children of the Europeans" and a promise to respect American property. McKeever then offered frightened settlers safety aboard *St. Louis,* and when Honi Heke attacked and destroyed the British fort, McKeever saved the fleeing garrison. He refused British pleas to land armed sailors to "save the day," insisting on American neutrality, but he did lead unarmed boats ashore under Maori fire to rescue civilians. As the Maoris burned everything except the Catholic mission and the American warehouses, *St. Louis* and two British ships rescued all the European settlers. Echoing American gratitude at Gibraltar, British Governor Robert Fitz Roy praised McKeever and his crew, saying "he sent his unarmed boats and went himself under frequent fire to [rescue] the women and children and convey them safely to his [ship]."

McKeever then returned his ship to Norfolk, where *St. Louis* spent the next three years out of service. In 1848 she joined the South American Squadron off Brazil just as Europe was being overwhelmed by a new wave of democratic and nationalistic uprisings and revolutions. Germany and the Austrian Empire were especially shaken by uprisings among minority nationalities, but the imperial army remained loyal and managed to suppress the revolutionaries. Many of these defeated revolutionaries, like millions of oppressed or unhappy people before and since, came to the United States. Called "Forty-Eighters," these new immigrants included Carl Schurz, later a Union general, senator from Missouri, and secretary of the interior, and two Hungarian patriots named Lajos Kossuth and Martin Koszta.

While many exiles came to the United States, others fled to havens closer to Europe, including Turkey and other parts of the crumbling Ottoman Empire. The Muslim Turks and Christian Austrians had been enemies for hundreds of years, and much of modern Yugoslavia and the Balkans remained Ottoman. Enemies of the Austrian Empire found a haven there, as they did in America. Kossuth came to the United States in December 1851 aboard the *Mississippi* at the invitation of Congress, and during his tour received an enthusiastic welcome in St. Louis where many Forty-Eighters had settled. Citizens of St. Louis urged Congress to give land to the Hungarian refugees, and Missourians named a town for Kossuth. His follower Martin Koszta had already immigrated and was working in New York City. In July 1852 Koszta declared his intention to become an American citizen.

Before he earned his citizenship, however, his employer sent him to Smyrna, Turkey, on business. There, he visited American consul Edward S. Offley, who cautioned him that because he was not yet a citizen, the consul could only "grant him . . . unofficial influence in case. . . of difficulties." Koszta nevertheless remained in Smyrna, where Austrian agents looking for "dangerous" revolutionaries spotted

The first *St. Louis* at Smyrna—challenging the Austrian Empire. (National Archives and Records Administration)

him. On June 22, 1853, he was kidnapped by the Austrians and dragged aboard the Austrian warship *Hussar* in chains. Exiles from Hungary, Italy, and other countries, as well as local American and British businessmen immediately protested to the American consul and the Turkish authorities, but they were powerless to rescue Koszta.

The next day, with Smyrna in an uproar over the kidnapping, an American warship arrived in the harbor. *St. Louis* had finished her service off South America, and in August 1852 had been assigned to the Mediterranean Squadron. Now commanded by Commander Duncan N. Ingraham of Charleston, South Carolina, she was about to play a central role in a major international crisis.

Koszta's outraged supporters immediately appealed to Commander Ingraham for help, and he and consul Offley visited *Hussar*, where they found Koszta in chains.

Ingraham demanded that the chains be removed, and he and the consul consulted by letter with the American minister in the Ottoman capital of Constantinople. All were aware that Koszta was not yet an American citizen; the Austrians considered him an Austrian subject. Local passions remained high. A mob attacked and murdered one of *Hussar*'s officers. At this point, an American congressman, Caleb Lyon of New York, arrived, and urged Ingraham "Do not let this chance slip to acquit yourself nobly and do honor to our country. . . .The eyes of nations are upon the little *St. Louis* and her commander." Ingraham also received an encouraging if vague letter from the American minister. He then returned to *Hussar* and formally asked Koszta: "Do you demand the protection of the American flag?" When Koszta said yes, Ingraham responded: "Then you shall have it."

On July 2, 1853, Commander Ingraham delivered an ultimatum to Captain August von Schwarz of *Hussar*: "[I] demand the person of Martin Koszta, a citizen of the United States . . . and if [refused, I will] take him by force." In spite of heavy odds against him, he then prepared *St. Louis* for battle against *Hussar* and two smaller Austrian warships. *St. Louis* midshipman Ralph Chandler, later an admiral, recorded in his diary: "every man on board seemed anxious for a fight. . . . We were all in a great state of excitement, but not an expression of fear or regret did I hear."

As Ingraham loaded his cannon, consul Offley warned the Austrian consul-general: "Ingraham is determined to go to the finish, and he is a professional fighting man. . . . Do you desire bloodshed?" Ten minutes before Ingraham's ultimatum expired, the Austrian consul-general ordered Captain von Schwarz to release his prisoner; Koszta was sent ashore into the custody of the local French consul.

In his report to the secretary of the navy, Commander Ingraham wrote:

I have taken a fearful responsibility upon me by this act;
but . . . could I have looked the American people in the face
again if I had allowed [Koszta] to be executed and not use
the power in my hands to protect him for fear of doing too
much?
. . . I . . . feel I have done my best to support the honor of
the flag, and not allowed a citizen to be oppressed who
claimed at my hand the protection of the flag.

He also wrote the American minister to Turkey: "and
now you gentlemen of the pen must uphold my act . . . as
[the Austrians] had more guns than I had . . . and three
[ships] to help them, they will not like to own it was fear
that made them deliver up Koszta."

Smyrna celebrated the rescue of Koszta with a great
party for Commander Ingraham and his officers, with
the "popping of bottle corks instead of the big guns," and
the local orchestra came out to *St. Louis* on a barge to ser-
enade the crew. Ironically, two days after *St. Louis* and
the Austrian ships had almost fought a bloody battle,
Hussar and her two Austrian sisters flew the Stars and
Stripes from their masts in honor of American Independence Day.

As with other such "diplomatic" naval actions before
transoceanic telegraph, the entire Koszta crisis was over
before news reached Washington. Still, the actions of the
American diplomats in Constantinople and Smyrna, and
Commander Ingraham's use of *St. Louis* to force an
ancient and powerful European empire to back down,
caused a sensation in Europe and America. Two weeks
after the crisis, on Bastille Day, the French national holiday, a Paris newspaper joyfully declared: "everyone who
has two free hands at the service of a noble heart will
applaud with frenzy this grand example given by the
new world to the old."

After the fact, the American government also approved,

and when Commander Ingraham returned to New York in September, he was showered with gifts and awards from Latin American and European exiles and patriots. He even received a costly naval chronometer from British working-men. In August 1854, Congress awarded him a gold medal and their "thanks. . . [for] his gallant and judicious conduct." Martin Koszta also returned to the United States, married a widow in Chicago, and went bankrupt trying to ranch near San Antonio, Texas. He apparently died in Guatemala in 1858, fighting with Central American guerrillas. Ingraham was promoted to captain and appointed commodore of the American squadron in the Mediterranean. In December 1860 his home state of South Carolina seceded from the Union, and in February 1861 he resigned his commission to join the new Confederate navy. A few months later the entire Mediterranean Squadron was recalled to America to fight in the Civil War. Although Ingraham had been prepared to risk his life to rescue a Hungarian exile in the name of the American flag, he joined three hundred of his fellow naval officers in renouncing the Stars and Stripes to serve the Confederacy.

St. Louis had remained in the Mediterranean Squadron until 1855, when she was transferred to the coast of Africa to join the British navy in suppressing the slave trade. The U.S. had outlawed the trade in African slaves in 1808, but huge profits inspired many unscrupulous sailors to continue the illegal trafficking. In 1858 *St. Louis* joined the Home Squadron in the Caribbean until the outbreak of the Civil War.

CHAPTER TWO

The Civil War—
Two American Navies

Another *St. Louis* and Another *Missouri*

Tension between the states over the issue of slavery had been growing even before slave-holding Missouri and free-state Maine joined the Union in the famous Missouri Compromise of 1821. Still, when southern states began seceding from the Union in December 1860, and Confederate President Jefferson Davis appointed Florida Senator Stephen Mallory Secretary of the Navy of the Confederate States of America in February 1861, the U.S. Navy was poorly prepared for war. Many senior officers had begun their service in the War of 1812 and had last seen battle over a decade before, against the Mexicans in 1846–1848. The navy's ships were small, old, and part of small squadrons scattered around the world. Almost half of the southern officers in the U.S. Navy resigned to fight for the Confederacy, including French Forrest, who had sailed *St. Louis* into San Francisco Bay in 1840, and Duncan Ingraham, who had rescued Martin Koszta from the Austrians in 1853. The Confederates also quickly captured navy shipyards at Norfolk, Virginia, and Pensacola, Florida, seizing hundreds of cannon and many naval supplies from these bases.

In spite of much early bungling, the Union entered the war with many advantages, including a much larger pop-

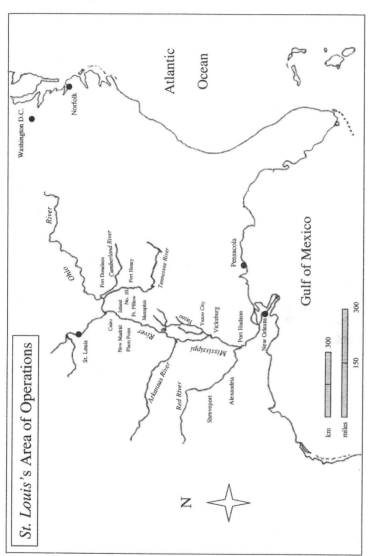

Strategic points in the Mississippi River valley during the Civil War.
(Courtesy Lieutenant Colonel Steve Oluic, Kent State University)

ulation and almost all the mines and factories needed to build the tools, weapons, and machines that this first modern technological war would demand. Finally, the Union had the benefit of a classic strategy: a blockade to cut the agricultural South off from foreign suppliers, and a plan to split and strangle the rebellion by capturing the rivers that divided the Confederacy. Thanks in large measure to powerful new unconventional ships built by a famous St. Louis riverman, the Union navy was able to seize crucial Southern strongholds along the Tennessee, Cumberland, Mississippi, and Red Rivers.

Before the Civil War, America had been content to lag behind Europe in many areas of military science and technology. Within five years, the Civil War had forced advancements in military and naval technology that made the Union navy for a brief time one of the largest and most powerful in the world. The South had no industry and few resources to build a modern armored steam navy. Confederate Secretary of the Navy Mallory relied upon the few tools at hand to build new types of weapons—ironclad warships, submarines, and explosive underwater mines (then called "torpedoes"). He also tried the classic American tactic of sending out fast commerce raiders like the *Alabama* and *Shenandoah,* captained by daring sailors like Raphael Semmes. Some two hundred Union merchant ships were taken during the war before the Federal navy captured or destroyed the raiders.

In January 1861, as state after southern state seceded from the Union, the sloop *St. Louis* was ordered to return from Vera Cruz, Mexico, to the Pensacola naval base. When Pensacola fell to the Rebels, *St. Louis* joined the navy ships enforcing the blockade. In September she helped the frigate *Brooklyn* capture the Confederate smuggler *Macao* off the Mississippi River. In February 1862, *St. Louis* was transferred to a new European Squadron. For the next two and a half years she patrolled the European and African

James Eads.
(Naval Historical Center)

coasts in search of Confederate commerce raiders. While *St. Louis* and her crew spent the Civil War on boring patrol, a second *St. Louis* would soon see more than her share of blood and death.

Many Missourians, including Governor Claiborne F. Jackson, supported the Confederacy, but Unionists controlled St. Louis. Among the strongest pro-Unionists was James B. Eads, who had made his fortune salvaging wrecked riverboats. He saw the strategic value of controlling the Mississippi, and well known for his enterprise and "hundred horsepower mouth," he traveled to Washington in April 1861 to urge President Lincoln to establish a strong naval base at the junction of the Mississippi and Ohio Rivers at Cairo, Illinois. U.S. army commander and Mexican War hero General Winfield Scott also favored an

James Eads's "City" gunboat *St. Louis.*
(Naval Historical Center)

"Anaconda Plan" to strangle the south with a blockade
and river campaign, and the famous U.S. Navy designer
Samuel Pook quickly drew up plans for ironclad gunboats
especially suited for river warfare. Secretary of the Navy
Gideon Welles recommended that these boats be built by
"western men. . . educated to the peculiar boat required for
navigating rivers." Eads was so eager to undertake the task
that he agreed to build seven boats in only three months
for ninety thousand dollars each, with a stiff penalty
should he be late.

He began work at the Carondelet boatyard near St. Louis
in August 1861 and soon had hundreds of Irish, French,
and German craftsmen and twelve sawmills working
around the clock. Although construction was delayed by
lack of guns and the tardiness of the government in pay-
ing Eads, the gunboats were launched in the fall of 1861
and moved downriver to Cairo to receive their guns and

crews. Christened *St. Louis, Carondelet, Louisville, Pittsburg, Mound City, Cairo*, and *Cincinnati*, the seven were known as "City" gunboats. Some 175 feet long and 50 feet wide, they were flat-bottomed, drew 7 feet of water, and had large center rear paddle wheels driven by coal-fueled steam engines. Each carried about a dozen guns and a crew of 175 officers and men. With a top speed of under nine miles an hour, they could sometimes barely move against a fast river current. Each engine burned some two thousand pounds of coal per hour and puffed loudly like railroad locomotives. Their chugging could be heard and their thick clouds of black coal smoke seen for miles up and down the river. The wooden ships' gundecks and pilothouses were armored with iron backed by two feet of thick oak. They were painted black with red hulls, and different color stripes on the smokestacks identified the ships. *St. Louis* wore yellow stripes. Their sailors called the gunboats "turtles" or "Pook's turtles" because they looked more like Mississippi mud turtles than ships or even riverboats.

In January 1862 the gunboats were accepted by Gunboat Flotilla commander Captain Andrew Hull Foote, although he still lacked crewmen. It was difficult to find volunteers among western rivermen. The *St. Louis Democrat* of January 24, 1862, reported: "The pay of the sailor [$18 per month] is somewhat more liberal than that of the soldier, and his duties include no long marches or wet encampments. He gets his meals with unfailing regularity and has always a dry bed—luxuries which a soldier can seldom count on."

Despite these advantages, Foote had to fill out his crews with untrained infantry and cavalry soldiers, landsmen, and even escaped or freed slaves. He warned his officers that soldiers "have hitherto led rather an irregular life, and had but few examples of well-disciplined people before their eyes. . . . Be strict. . . treat them kindly, but let them feel they must conform to naval laws."

A month later Foote and the army commander in Cairo, Brigadier General Ulysses S. Grant, aggressively penetrated the heart of the Confederacy. From their Cairo base, Foote's gunboats and Grant's troops moved up the Ohio River to attack Fort Henry on the Tennessee River near the Kentucky-Tennessee border. On February 6, 1862, with sisters *Cincinnati, Carondelet,* and *St. Louis* leading the attack, Foote steamed slowly up to Fort Henry and bombarded the fortification for over an hour until Confederate General Lloyd Tilghman surrendered his troops. The new "brown water" navy thus captured a fortified rebel garrison with no help from ground troops. In the exchange of cannon fire, Foote's flagship *Cincinnati* was hit thirty-one times but only suffered one sailor killed. *St. Louis* and *Carondelet* took more than a half-dozen hits each but suffered no casualties. In contrast, the converted riversteamer *Essex* was hit in the boiler, and the resulting explosion killed ten and wounded twenty-three.

Foote's fleet adopted General Tilghman's pet dog, "Ponto," as spoils of this first victory. Ponto seemingly shifted allegiance and "left no doubt of [his] political [views.] If the sailors called him 'Jeff Davis,' Ponto would howl dolefully. If called 'Abe Lincoln,' he'd bark joyfully."

Exploiting his first success, Foote pressed upriver, capturing Confederate steamboats and supplies and destroying railroad lines. Within a week, Foote and Grant attacked Fort Donelson on the Cumberland River. Many rebel troops had escaped Fort Henry to reinforce Fort Donelson. The navy now learned the hard lesson that the Confederates had taught the Union army at Bull Run near Washington—this war would be a long, painful struggle. Foote led the gunboat attack on February 14 in *St. Louis.* Both *St. Louis* and *Louisville* were crippled by heavy fire, and Foote, along with many of his crew, was injured when a shell hit *St. Louis*'s wheelhouse. A cannon burst on *Carondelet,* and *Pittsburg* and other gunboats were also heavily damaged.

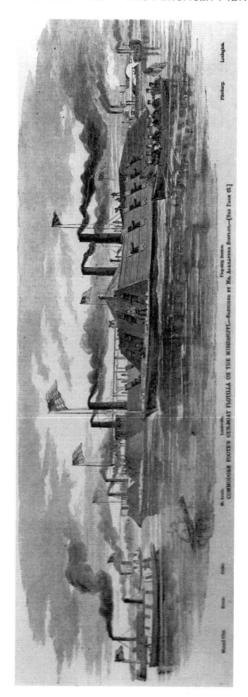

The Union Mississippi River Flotilla. (Naval Historical Center)

Confederate cannonballs broke through iron plating, sending deadly wood splinters flying inside the boats. Other balls entered gunports, killing and wounding until the decks were slippery with blood. Although the boilers were padded with sandbags, some balls penetrated the boilers, scalding crewmen with steam. Battered and drifting, the fleet was forced to withdraw. The Union army then attacked; 500 Union soldiers were killed and 2,100 wounded. Although many rebels escaped, Major General Simon Buckner decided to surrender his 9,000 remaining troops and asked for terms. Grant replied that he would accept "no terms except unconditional and immediate surrender." Buckner wrote back that "the overwhelming force under your command compel me, notwithstanding the brilliant success of the Confederate arms . . . to accept [your] ungenerous and unchivalrous terms."

The Union navy had only fifty-four men killed or wounded, including Foote himself, but the fleet had been battered and had to withdraw to Cairo for repairs. *St. Louis* had been hit by fifty-nine cannonballs. Nevertheless, the Union now controlled the Tennessee and Cumberland River valleys and could quickly move gunboats and troops by water. Nashville soon fell to the Union.

An army of twenty-five thousand men under Union Brigadier General John Pope captured New Madrid, Missouri, in early March 1862, but the Mississippi was blocked by heavy Confederate fortifications on Island Number 10 in the middle of the river. Foote was suffering severe pain from his wound, but he moved his flotilla down from Cairo to support Pope's army. On March 17, while *St. Louis* was bombarding the Confederate batteries on Island Number 10, one of her guns exploded, killing two and wounding ten of her crew. As a fellow captain complained, this was "another proof . . . that the guns furnished the Western Flotilla were less destructive of the enemy than to ourselves." After two more weeks stalled by the guns on the island, *Carondelet* ran past the Confederate batteries during a thunderstorm on the night of April 4. Two nights later *Pittsburg* also braved the guns and joined her sister at New Madrid. Protected by these two iron-clads, General Pope's army crossed the river into Kentucky without losing a man. Surrounded, the Confederates on Island Number 10 surrendered five thousand soldiers and one hundred cannon.

Pope and Foote immediately pushed seventy-five miles farther downriver toward Memphis until they were again blocked by Fort Pillow on the Tennessee bluffs. There the advance stalled as Pope's troops were diverted to support an attack on Corinth, Mississippi.

The navy was not idle though. At the mouth of the Mississippi, Flag Officer David G. Farragut commanded a fleet of big oceangoing warships, including the old *Mississippi.* In early April, Farragut moved his ships upriver toward New Orleans, dragging *Mississippi* over sandbars to reach deeper water. On April 18 his mortarboats under Captain David Dixon Porter began bombarding Forts Jackson and St. Phillip below New Orleans. On April 24 he steamed his fleet past the forts, and the next day Union troops reoccupied the Federal buildings in New Orleans and recaptured the city.

Two weeks later Flag Officer Foote, fearing that the pain of his wound was clouding his judgment, turned over command of his gunboat flotilla, sitting above Fort Pillow, to Captain Charles Henry Davis. Davis was shocked at the toll that the wound and war had taken on his friend, finding him "fallen off in flesh and depressed in spirits." The next day, Sunday, May 10, the Confederate army's "Mississippi River Defense Fleet," eight rams clad in protective bales of cotton, surprised the Union fleet as it was lazily shelling Fort Pillow. The rebels were commanded by Captain James Montgomery and Missouri guerrilla General Jeff Thompson. Only one Union mortarboat was on duty, and her "escort," *Cincinnati*, lay nearby with cold boilers and no power to move as her crew scrubbed her decks. Her sisters were too far upstream to help her as the rebel rams suddenly appeared around a bend in the river. *Cincinnati* was quickly rammed by three Confederate boats. Her guns did severe damage to the lightly protected Southern rams, but her captain was badly wounded and, with boilers and ammunition magazine flooded, she sank to the bottom. By now *Carondelet* and *Mound City* were coming to *Cincinnati's* aid. *Mound City* was also rammed and ran aground to keep from sinking, but *Carondelet* and another Union ironclad chased the Southern rams back to the shelter of Fort Pillow's guns. *Cairo* and *St. Louis*, moored across the river and blinded by morning haze, were never able to join the fight. The battle of Plum Run Bend was a real setback to the Union flotilla, caught by surprise and heavily damaged by the Southern rams. Montgomery bragged that the Union "will never penetrate farther down the Mississippi."

Cincinnati and *Mound City* were raised from the river bottom and towed back to Cairo for repairs, and the Union flotilla sat above Fort Pillow waiting for Union rams to come downriver to match their enemy. On May 25 the seven steamers of Colonel Charles Ellet's U.S. Army Mississippi Ram Fleet arrived, and Ellet urged Davis to attack Fort Pillow at once. The Confederate army withdrew from Corinth, however, and left Fort Pillow exposed. The garrison blew up the fort and escaped downriver on Montgomery's defense fleet to make a stand at Memphis.

Union forces followed, and by early June Davis's ironclads, Ellet's rams, and army troop transports had reached Memphis and were facing the Confederate River Defense Fleet. At dawn on June 6, as crowds of Memphis citizens watched from the riverbanks, Davis's ironclads *Carondelet*, *Louisville*, *Cairo*, *St. Louis*, and *Benton* lined up facing the Confederate rams. Suddenly, Ellet steamed his flagship,

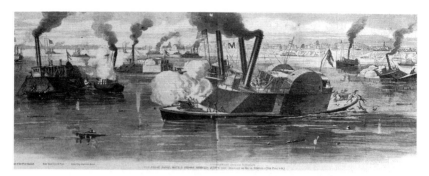

The Battle of Memphis. (Naval Historical Center)

Queen of the West, through the ironclad fleet, to the cheers of their crews, and charged the rebels. Captain Henry Walke of *Carondelet* watched as "the rams rushed upon each other like wild beasts in deadly combat." In the chaos and smoke of exploding and sinking Southern rams, the Union ironclads joined the fight, and the Confederate fleet was overwhelmed. Only one ram managed to escape to join the Southern defenders at Vicksburg. General Jeff Thompson watched the destruction of his frail cottonclads from the shore, and according to Captain Walke, commented "they are gone and I am going" as he mounted his horse and left the citizens of Memphis to the Union army.

The Union now held Memphis, the fifth-largest Confederate city with its huge store of cotton, its four railroad lines, and its Confederate navy shipyard, which Davis took over to repair and resupply the fleet. While in Memphis, Davis ordered *St. Louis* and *Mound City,* along with the Forty-sixth Indiana Infantry Regiment, up the Arkansas and White Rivers into the state of Arkansas to search for Southern gunboats. On June 17 the gunboats and infantry attacked Southern fortifications on the White at St. Charles. Sunken hulks in the rivers forced the two ironclads to advance single file. *Mound City,* in the lead, was hit in the main steam drum, and scalding steam filled the boat. As the surviving crew jumped into the river to escape, Southern sharpshooters "commenced murdering those who were struggling in the water, and also firing upon those in our boats sent to pick them up." The outraged Forty-sixth Indiana silenced the snipers and seized the fort, but *Mound City*'s agony was not yet over.

When John Duble from *Conestoga* went aboard *Mound City* to relieve her wounded captain:

> I beheld with extreme disgust a portion of the few men who were unwounded, drunk. A portion of the crew of *St. Louis* [and other sailors and soldiers] were in the same beastly condition. . . . Men while lying in the agonies of death were robbed. . . . Rooms were broken into, trunks pillaged . . . and destroyed. Watches of the officers were stolen, and quarreling, cursing, and rioting, as well as robbing, seemed to rule. . . . Not the first particle of order was observed. . . . While our doctor and nurses were rendering all relief in their power to the suffering, a portion of the crews seemed bent on destruction and theft. I hope never again . . . to see so much misery, such depravity, and so much disorder.

Duble recovered and buried fifty-nine of *Mound City*'s dead, but out of a crew of 175, some 82 had been killed in the steam explosion, 43 shot in the water, and another 24 scalded or otherwise wounded.

As the river level dropped and the gunboats repeatedly ran aground, *St. Louis* escorted her crippled sister *Mound City* to Memphis for repairs. Growing numbers of rebel snipers and guerrilla bands harassed the Forty-sixth Indiana, and the problem of guerrilla sharpshooters became so severe that on October 18, 1862, Rear Admiral David Dixon Porter issued a general order to the whole flotilla.

When any of our vessels are fired on, it will be the duty of the commander to fire back with spirit and to destroy everything in that neighborhood within reach of his guns. There is no impropriety in destroying houses [suspected of] affording shelter to rebels and it is the only way to stop guerrilla warfare. Should innocent persons suffer, it will be their own fault, and teach others that it will be to their advantage to inform the Government authorities when guerrillas are about.

At the end of June, Flag Officer Farragut invited Captain Davis to help attack Vicksburg, the last Confederate stronghold on the Mississippi. Davis told Secretary of the Navy Welles, "I leave at the earliest possible moment." A month before Farragut had arrived from New Orleans with his warships and demanded that the city's defenders surrender. The Confederates refused, and Union forces spent the next thirteen months trying to crack this last great rebel Mississippi River fortress. Davis's flotilla arrived from Memphis on the first of July, but since most army troops had been ordered to Tennessee and Kentucky, the ironclads were stalled at anchor north of the town and its strong fortifications. As the hot, miserable southern summer dragged on, the Union sailors dropped from malaria and dysentery. According to *Carondelet*'s captain, his crew of "Northmen, considered the hardiest race in the world, melted away in the Southern sun with surprising rapidity." Fortunately, the Union found a ready source of replacements. As the navy's General Orders directed: "Owing to the increasing sickness in the Squadron, and the scarcity of men, it becomes necessary . . . to use . . . . contrabands. . . . [B]lacks will make efficient men. . . . The policy of the Government is to use the blacks, and every officer should do his utmost to carry this policy out."

The decreasing number of healthy skilled sailors was not Farragut's only worry. The water level of the Mississippi

River was dropping so fast that his big seagoing ships could be stranded.

Vicksburg was protected by high bluffs and a maze of swamps, bayous, and rivers such as the Yazoo to the north and Big Black to the south. The Union navy's great advantage was that gunboats, troops, and supplies could move with relative ease and speed by water while soldiers struggled with muddy roads or trails, thick swamps, and heavy forests. But the rivers also harbored Southern threats such as powerful ironclad rams. The South could not hope to match the size of the North's fleets, but when Farragut stormed New Orleans in April he had faced the guns of the Confederate *Manassas* and the unfinished *Louisiana* and *Mississippi*. The Union fleet captured or destroyed all three. When Davis's gunboats beat Montgomery's rams at Memphis in June, the Confederate ram *Tennessee* was burned. Another unfinished ironclad ram, *Arkansas*, escaped from Memphis, and was dragged one hundred miles up the Yazoo River to Greenwood, Mississippi, to safety. Confederate navy Commander Isaac Newton Brown scraped together ten guns, found some iron to protect the front of the boat, and recruited a crew from the survivors of General Jeff Thompson's Missouri guerrillas. While he struggled to complete *Arkansas*, Vicksburg commander General Earl Van Dorn urged him to attack the Union fleet. "It is better to die game . . . than to lie by and be burned up in the Yazoo."

On July 15, 1862, Farragut ordered Davis to scout the Yazoo, and the ironclad *Carondelet*, wooden steamer *Tyler*, and ram *Queen of the West* started up the river. Without warning, they ran into *Arkansas* coming down. *Carondelet* was badly shot up and run aground. *Arkansas* chased the two light Union boats toward the Mississippi, but the fleeing *Tyler* managed to damage *Arkansas* so badly that when she finally reached the Mississippi, her engines could barely move her. Although they should have been warned by noise of the running battle, Farragut's crews were caught unprepared; the ships had cold boilers and no steam to power their engines. The crippled *Arkansas* drifted downstream through the anchored Union fleet. Union cannons blazed away, but *Arkansas* survived and finally ran aground at Vicksburg. The furious and embarrassed Farragut sent his rams to try to destroy *Arkansas,* but she remained a dangerous threat.

As the river level dropped sixteen feet, Farragut gave up and moved his big ships back downriver in late July while Davis moved his ironclads upriver to Memphis. Vickburg remained in Southern hands. Indeed, the Confederates were so confident that in early August *Arkansas* and Major General John Breckinridge's troops moved down to attack weak Union forces at Baton Rouge, Louisiana. *Arkansas*'s engines repeatedly failed, and she was destroyed by Union gunboats. Still, the Union forces withdrew from Baton Rouge. The Confederates again held the river from Vicksburg south. To block any new Union naval attack, they sent sixteen thousand troops to fortify the bluffs at Port Hudson, Louisiana.

After a successful spring in which the Union gunboats had moved south past Memphis and the Union fleet had advanced north past New Orleans, the summer of 1862 ended with the Confederates still holding the key to the Mississippi River valley. Congress created the new rank of rear admiral and promoted both Farragut and Foote. Davis became commodore of the U.S. Navy Mississippi River Squadron and was replaced in September by Acting Rear Admiral David Dixon Porter, Farragut's foster brother.

Also in September 1862, since the U.S. Navy already had one *St. Louis* on patrol in the Atlantic off Europe, Eads's City ironclad *St. Louis* was renamed *Baron de Kalb.* John, Baron de Kalb, a Bavarian soldier, had come to America with Lafayette during the Revolution to help fight the British. Appointed a major general in the Continental Army, he had been fatally wounded in the Battle of Camden, New Jersey, in August 1780.

The newly named *Baron de Kalb* stayed with her iron-clad sisters and continued to play an important role in the battle for Vicksburg. In October, Ulysses S. Grant was made commander of the U.S. Army's Department of the Tennessee, and in December, Porter's ironclads escorted eighty-five transport boats carrying General William Tecumseh Sherman's army back toward Vicksburg to renew the battle. Looking for a way around the heavily fortified town and bluffs, Porter sent *Baron de Kalb, Cairo,* and *Pittsburg* back up the Yazoo. The boats moved slowly, their crews clearing logjams and Confederate "torpedoes," but on December 12, 1862, *Cairo* became the first ship in history to be destroyed by an electrical mine. Confederate sailors Zedekiah McDaniel and Francis Ewing were lying in ambush on the riverbank and set off two mines that sank *Cairo* in twelve minutes in thirty-six feet of water. (*Cairo* would lie on the bottom of the Yazoo for one hundred years. She was raised in the 1960s, and today this last surviving City gunboat is preserved at the Vicksburg National Military Park.)

Two weeks after the sinking of *Cairo, Baron de Kalb* again steamed up the Yazoo to destroy rebel shipping. After being blocked by winter weather and impassable swamps, the ironclads tried the Yazoo again in late February 1863. *Baron de Kalb* and *Chillicothe* led a group of transports with forty-five hundred soldiers up the Yazoo. Harassed by snipers, the sailors and troops slowly cleared logs and moved the fleet up to Greenwood, Mississippi, where on March 10, 1863, they were blocked by Fort Pemberton. *Chillicothe* was crippled by cannon fire, but *Baron de Kalb* returned fire and heavily damaged the fort; however, swamps prevented the Union troops from capturing the fort, and the expedition retreated in "miserable failure."

The very next day Admiral Farragut brought his warships back up the Mississippi to Baton Rouge. To get to Vicksburg to join Grant and Porter, Farragut now had to brave the twisting river and powerful batteries at Port Hudson. On the evening of March 14, he led his fleet up to Port Hudson and disaster. Of Farragut's big ships, only the flagship, *Hartford,* made it safely to Vicksburg. The old paddle wheeler *Mississippi,* sister to the first *Missouri,* ran hard aground under the merciless Confederate fire. Lieutenant George Dewey, who was to destroy the Spanish fleet in Manila Bay in 1898 to help win the Philippines for America, was second in command. Although he tried, he could not free the ship from the sandbar. The *Mississippi's* crew set her afire so the Confederates could not capture her, and as she slid off the sandbar and sank, the heat of the flames caused her guns to fire. Dewey described her as "a dying ship manned by dead men, firing on the enemy."

Even without Farragut's big ships, the navy continued to support Grant's advance on Vicksburg. As Grant moved his army south through Louisiana past Vicksburg looking for a place to cross the Mississippi, Porter moved *Carondelet, Pittsburg, Mound City,* and *Louisville* south to bombard Grand Gulf and cover the troops' crossing. After suffering many hits from the powerful Grand Gulf batteries, the ironclads had to withdraw. *Baron de Kalb* had remained north of Vicksburg and escorted General William T. Sherman's troops back up the Yazoo to distract the Confederates while Grant crossed the Mississippi and marched on the state capital at Jackson.

By mid-May, Jackson had fallen to Grant. On May 18, *Baron de Kalb* shelled Haines Bluff on the Yazoo as the Rebels fell back to join General John Pemberton's twenty thousand defenders in Vicksburg. While the army surrounded Vicksburg and Port Hudson, navy mortarboats shelled the defenders. A Southern soldier reported that inside the tightening Union ring, the troops ate "all the beef—all the mules—all the dogs—all the rats."

On July 4, 1863, Vicksburg fell. Porter was made permanent rear admiral, and one thousand miles away in Pennsylvania, Robert E. Lee began his long retreat from Gettysburg. Port Hudson fell on July 9, and as President Lincoln said, "the father of waters again flowed unvexed to the sea." General Sherman congratulated Porter: "the day of our nation's birth is consecrated and baptized anew in a victory won by the united navy and army." On July 13, 1863, Secretary of the Navy Welles wrote: " To yourself, your officers, and brave and gallant sailors who have been so . . . persistent and enduring through many months of trial and hardship, and so daring . . . I tender, in the name of the President, the thanks and congratulations of the whole country."

On the very day that Welles wrote with his congratulations, *Baron de Kalb* steamed up to the burning rebel shipyard at Yazoo City and hit two mines placed by Confederates in the Yazoo River. Although the crew suffered no casualties and were able to salvage the guns, the bow and stern were shattered; the *Baron de Kalb* could not be recovered. As late as 1930, her wreckage could be seen in the river at low water.

From the beginning of the war it had been clear that the Confederacy could not hope to match the Union in population, wealth, or industry, nor could the Confederate navy compete with the Union navy. Still, both the Union and the Confederacy showed that ironclad gunboats could be effective warships in inland rivers and protected harbors. Eads's City gunboats helped the Union army reclaim the Mississippi Valley, and *Virginia* had almost broken the Union blockade of Norfolk. Confederate Secretary of the Navy Stephen Mallory concentrated his limited resources on these small and fairly simple river and harbor ironclads and, to protect his shipbuilding efforts from Northern attack, established primitive inland shipyards in such river towns as Richmond; Columbus, Georgia; Selma and Montgomery, Alabama; Yazoo City, Mississippi; and Shreveport, Louisiana, up small rivers far from Union forces.

By October 1862, with the Union blockade in place and Grant, Sherman, Porter, and Farragut preparing to again attack Vicksburg, Mallory had eighteen ironclads under construction. Although James Eads had faced great difficulties in building and arming his City gunboats a year earlier, his problems were simple compared to the challenges facing Mallory and his officers. In Shreveport, Louisiana, up the shallow and twisting Red River, Lieutenant Jonathan H. Carter signed a contract on November 1, 1862, for an ironclad to be completed in six months at a cost of 336,000 Confederate dollars (over three times the dollar cost of Eads's City ironclads.)

Carter raced to finish his gunboat while Vicksburg still held out against the Union army and navy, and Secretary Mallory encouraged his officers to show energy and initiative: "You are a long ways from [the Confederate capital of] Richmond and must not hesitate to take responsibility. . . . Your . . . labors will be onerous."

He did not exaggerate. Confederate navy officers were forced to compete with one another and with the Confederate army for supplies and men. They begged local army commanders for skilled carpenters, and Carter even "kidnapped" soldiers home on leave from the war. They built their boats of green unseasoned timber caulked with cotton and could scarcely find even such simple supplies as nails, pots and pans, and hammocks. Because Southern mills could not produce enough armor plating, Carter bought rails from railroads in the north Louisiana towns of Monroe, Alexandria, and Shreveport for his boat. By February 1863, as Union troops were throwing themselves against Vicksburg's defenses, Carter's boat was almost ready for its armor. He suggested naming the boat *Caddo* in honor of a local Indian tribe, but Mallory christened her *Missouri*. The Confederate *Missouri* was launched into the

Red River on April 14, just a month after Admiral Farragut lost the Union *Missouri*'s sister *Mississippi* at Port Hudson.

Carter worried that the Red River was falling so low that his unfinished gunboat would be stranded. He considered moving downriver to Alexandria, although there his unarmored and unarmed gunboat would have been in danger of attack by Porter's Union fleet. The battle of Vicksburg was growing more desperate, and General Pemberton had taken *Missouri*'s guns to strengthen his batteries at Grand Gulf. These guns helped beat off Porter's gunboats, forcing Grant to move farther south to cross the Mississippi River to attack Jackson, Mississippi, and surround Vicksburg.

Missouri was now the only Confederate ironclad left in the Mississippi Valley, and Carter finally got two powerful naval guns from a captured Union gunboat. *Missouri* was officially turned over to the Confederate navy by her Shreveport builders in September, two months after the fall of Vicksburg, but her guns were not in place until December 1863. Looking very much like Eads's City ironclads, *Missouri* was 183 feet long and 53 feet wide. Her armored casement to house her guns and protect her crew and machinery was built of timber two feet thick covered with about four and a half inches of railroad rails. She had two engines salvaged from river steamboats driving a 22-foot paddle wheel, but her top speed was only a disappointing six miles per hour. Badly armed, weakly armored, poorly built, underpowered, leaky, and slow, *Missouri* was also stranded far up a shallow and difficult river from the vastly more powerful enemy fleet. Her first captain, Lieutenant Commander Charles M. Fauntleroy, was so horrified at his new boat that he ungratefully told the long-suffering and hardworking Lieutenant Carter that "he hoped the damned boat would sink . . . he never intended to serve in her if he could help it."

Fauntleroy soon departed, leaving Carter in command of the Red River Squadron of *Missouri* and the fast wooden steam ram *Webb*. Like Union Mississippi Squadron commander Captain Andrew Foote two years earlier, Carter now faced the problem of finding a crew for his new ironclad. He had earlier begged the army for craftsmen and guns; now he begged for crewmen. The army was of course reluctant to give up able-bodied soldiers, and in January 1864, Carter warned General Kirby Smith "should the time come when *Missouri*'s services will be required and no men on board, the fault will not be mine." The army finally sent some cannoneers, but these men objected to performing the other duties expected of sailors, complaining that they only had orders to work the guns. Many soon returned to their army units, leaving *Missouri* again shorthanded.

Carter's warning to General Smith had been prophetic, for indeed the Union was planning a major attack up the Red River. Kirby Smith also predicted a Union attack up the Red and Ouachita Rivers before the rivers dropped too low for Porter's fleet, and he ordered Carter to move *Missouri* down to Alexandria to support him. Both Secretary Mallory and General Smith were expecting *Missouri* to challenge the massed strength of Porter's fleet, fresh from the victory at Vicksburg and the conquest of the entire Mississippi River.

The Battle of Memphis was the Mississippi River Squadron's most decisive victory, and the Battle of Vicksburg was a wonderful example of army-navy cooperation. The Red River campaign of 1864 was almost the navy's worst disaster. Union politicians and ambitious army officers wanted to seize Louisiana and Texas, in large part because of their rich stores of cotton. Admiral Porter agreed to support the army with his Mississippi Squadron once the Red River rose high enough in the spring to float his vessels. Along with lightly armored "tinclads" and two advanced Eads turret monitors, his fleet included City ironclads *Mound City, Carondelet, Pittsburg*, and *Louisville*.

Easily reaching the prosperous central Louisiana town of Alexandria, Porter confidently wrote:

> The efforts of these people [the Confederates] to keep up this war remind me very much of the antics of Chinamen, who build canvas forts, paint hideous dragons on their shields, turn somersets and yell in the faces of their enemies to frighten them, and then run away at the first sign of an engagement. . . . It is not the intention of these rebels to fight.

His sailors put their time in Alexandria to good use. Under regulations then in effect the army had to take possession of "enemy" cotton on behalf of the U.S. treasury. The navy, on the other hand, could seize it as a "prize of war," with 50 percent of the profit going to the naval personnel involved, and 5 percent to Porter himself. To the outrage of the army, sailors even made up fake "Confederate States of America" stencils, painted the label on cotton bales, added "U.S. Navy" underneath, and loaded the "captured" bales on their ships. Admiral Porter was amused when an army colonel told him that "C.S.A./ U.S.N." stood for "cotton-stealing association of the U.S. Navy." His gunboat crews received a quarter million dollars in prize money, and Porter personally got over twelve thousand dollars.

General Grant urged the army and navy to advance toward Shreveport and the waiting *Missouri*, but for the first time in a decade, the Red was failing to rise quickly enough for most of Porter's fleet to clear the rapids above Alexandria. In early April, Porter dragged his flagship, *Eastport*, and eleven other gunboats, including his four "Cities" over the falls and moved upriver escorting thirty transports. As the boats passed piles of burning cotton, they were greeted by slaves from riverbank plantations. A soldier noted in his diary: "One group of color'd girls welcomed us with waving of handkerchiefs, bonnets and aprons and a song and a hurra for Lincoln too. . . . . '[It was a great day] when de Linkum gunboats come.'"

Despite low water and occasional groundings, the fleet quickly reached Springfield Landing some thirty miles south of Shreveport and Carter's *Missouri*. At that point, Porter

> found a sight that made me laugh. It was the smartest thing I ever knew the rebels to do. They had gotten that huge steamer *New Falls River* across Red River. . . 15 feet of her on shore on each side, the boat broken in the middle and a sandbar [forming under her]. An invitation in large letters to attend a ball in Shreveport was kindly stuck up by the rebels, [but] we were never able to accept.

Porter then learned that the Union army had been defeated and was retreating toward Alexandria, leaving him and his fleet stuck in the narrow, shallow river surrounded by Rebel troops. The retreat was a nightmare as boats ran aground, hit sunken logs and stumps, and broke rudders or paddle wheels. Porter was forced to blow up his flagship to keep it out of Rebel hands, and shortly thereafter two transports were ambushed. One was carrying 175 "contraband" former slaves from upriver plantations, and almost all were scalded to death by escaping steam when her boiler was hit.

Porter's battered fleet and exhausted crews reached Alexandria again at the end of April, where they discovered that the water over the falls was only three feet deep—less than half the seven feet of water needed to get his gunboats to safety. The navy feared that the army might abandon them and force Porter to destroy his Mississippi River Squadron to prevent its capture. Fortunately, among the soldiers was a Wisconsin engineer, Lieutenant Colonel Joseph Bailey, who had served at Vicksburg and

Port Hudson and had years of experience with shallow rivers. He proposed to build a dam to raise the water level enough for the fleet to clear the falls. Porter was skeptical, and punned "if you can dam better than I can you must be a good hand at it, for I have been 'damning' all night." Still, the prospect of losing his fleet and facing professional ruin humbled him, and he assured the army "if he . . . can get me out of this scrape, I'll be eternally grateful." The Union general responded that "Colonel Bailey has been ordered to build the dam with all energy and vigor in his power."

The challenge before Bailey seemed impossible. Porter's gunboats faced two sets of falls with a total drop of 13 feet in a river 760 feet wide with a nine-mile-an-hour current. Despite widespread pessimism and gloom, Bailey organized 3,000 troops, 200 wagons, and 1,000 horses, mules, and oxen for the project. Troops cut down an entire forest on the northern, or Pineville, bank, and gathered lumber and rubble from Alexandria for materials to build the dam. The troops worked through the nights by the light of bonfires, and suffered through hot Louisiana days with little clean drinking water, as the Red was polluted with human and animal bodies. Soldiers and sailors risked drowning in the rushing river. Meanwhile, with some 6,000 men, the Confederates surrounded and trapped 31,000 U.S. troops. The Confederates also ambushed gunboats and troop transports between Alexandria and the safety of the Mississippi River. In the ten days needed to build Bailey's dam and free the fleet, the Union lost 2 gunboats, 3 transports, and 600 men.

By May 8, the lighter monitors and gunboats had cleared the upper falls, but the army complained that the navy would not do enough to lighten the gunboats, such as abandon their heavy loads of captured cotton. On May 9 the rising river burst Bailey's dam, and the unprepared navy was only able to get four gunboats through the rushing flood. All four "Cities" were left stranded above the

Porter's fleet passing Bailey's dam on the Red River.
(Naval Historical Center)

falls. Finally, Porter's sailors began working seriously. As the army built new dams, the gunboat crews unloaded guns and heavy supplies and even threw their iron armor into the river, painting the bare wooden sides of the boats black to fool the Confederates.

In their next try, *Carondelet* and *Mound City* stuck fast in the upper falls, but 3,000 troops dragged them clear. They then faced the rushing torrent of the lower falls, a "wild looking place to run a large gunboat into." *Mound City* was the first City to brave the falls. Her crew sealed her gunports and ran the flood while thousands watched and army bands on shore played "The Star-Spangled Banner" and "The Battle Cry of Freedom." The gunboat hit bottom and dragged and twisted through the rushing "niagara." As the whole boat groaned and twisted, her crew was terrified that her steam joints might break and fill the sealed boat with deadly steam; they remembered that over a hundred of their crewmates had been killed on June 17, 1862, when her boiler was hit during the battle with the Confederate fort at St. Charles, Arkansas, on the White River. To the cheers of the watching crowd, *Mound City* survived the wild ride, and by May 13 *Carondelet, Pittsburg,* and *Louisville* were also clear.

General Joseph Bailey.
(National Archives and
Records Administration)

As Union forces left Alexandria, arsonists set fires that swept the town, leaving the population homeless. The gunboats led the retreat south, shelling the treeline along the river to discourage Confederate attacks. By May 18, Porter wrote his mother, "I am clear of my troubles and my fleet is safe out in the broad Mississippi. I have had a hard and anxious time of it."

Congress formally thanked Lieutenant Colonel Bailey and gave him a gold medal. Porter personally gave him a beautiful sword, and his naval officers gave him a silver punch bowl. He ended the war a brigadier general and then settled on a farm in Vernon County, Missouri. Elected sheriff, he was murdered on March 21, 1867, by two prisoners he was taking to jail.

The Red River campaign was a near disaster for Porter's fleet. Between December 1864 and April 1865 Congress held hearings on the campaign, concluding that the "only results, in addition to the disasters that attended it, were of a commercial and political nature." One ironclad captain called the navy's experience "one of the most humiliating and disastrous that had to be recorded during the war." Lieutenant Carter never got into the fight as *Missouri* remained stranded at Shreveport because of shallow water dowstream. Finally, in January 1865, Carter received army recruits to fill out his crew: "wild Texans and men who have never seen a gun or ship." At the end of March, the Red rose enough for *Missouri* to move downstream. Carter wrote the Confederate general in command: " I will . . . be pleased to welcome you on the deck of the *Missouri*. . . . I hope to be a valuable [addition] . . . to your forces defending the [Red River] valley."

On April 8, *Missouri* reached Confederate forts at the rapids above Alexandria. The next day, Robert E. Lee surrendered to Ulysses S. Grant at Appomattox in Virginia. On May 2, Confederate Secretary of the Navy Stephen Mallory resigned as President Jefferson Davis fled from Richmond. At the end of May, Union Lieutenant Commander W. E. Fitzhugh brought a small Union flotilla upriver to take possession of Confederate navy personnel and property on the Red. He

> met no resistance whatever . . . and [on June 3, 1865] met Lieutenant-Commanding J. H. Carter, commanding Naval Forces, Trans-Mississippi Department, and received from him the ironclad *Missouri* [and the surrender of his] officers and men . . . . *Missouri* . . . is a very formidable vessel, plated with railroad iron. She . . . leaks badly, and . . . is very slow.

Missouri was brought to Mound City, Illinois, to join the ironclads of the Union Mississippi River Squadron being dismantled. Along with the surviving City ironclads

Carondelet, Louisville, Mound City, and *Pittsburg,* she was disarmed and decommissioned. At the end of November, *Missouri* was sold for scrap for $2,100. Although never firing a shot in anger, *Missouri* had the distinction of being the last Confederate ship to surrender on American territory.

The Union Mississippi Squadron, once one hundred ships strong, was dissolved on August 14, 1865, and only *Cairo* remains of Eads's seven City ironclads. From their very first action against Forts Henry and Donelson it was clear that *St. Louis* and her sisters were quite vulnerable. Heavy cannonballs sent wooden splinters flying around the gundeck or entered gunports to knock over guns, kill crewmen, or burst machinery and release scalding steam. The armored pilothouses were often hit, killing or injuring skilled river pilots or commanding officers. The slow and clumsy boats could be rammed by faster Confederate cotton-clad river rams or overwhelmed by more powerful Confederate ironclads like *Arkansas.* Finally, they could be sunk by mines in the narrow western rivers. Rear Admiral David Dixon Porter, who commanded them at Vicksburg and almost lost them at Alexandria, recognized that they were "temporary expedients" that "suffered a great deal." Still, they proved sturdy and dependable. As Porter said: "No vessels have done harder fighting anywhere. . . . Some of them have been sunk and others badly cut up, but they have seldom failed to achieve their objectives, and have opened or have helped to open, over 3500 miles of river once in the hands of the enemy."

CHAPTER THREE

The Great Naval Arms Race and the First World War

Decline and Rebirth— A New *Missouri* and Two Named *St. Louis*

At the end of the Civil War the United States had the most experienced, most powerful army and navy in the world, but within two years hundreds of ships had been cut from the huge 671 ship wartime fleet. In 1865 the navy had 7,000 officers and 51,500 men, but by December 1867 only 2,000 officers, 12,000 men, and 103 ships remained. When David Farragut died in 1870, David Dixon Porter became senior admiral of the navy until his own death in 1890, and the U.S. Navy returned to the comfortable prewar practice of using tiny American squadrons to protect American commercial interests around the world.

The American navy had experimented with many technological advances, and steam power, armor, gun turrets, naval guns, and ammunition had quickly improved in the laboratory of a four-year war. European naval experts had watched the American experience with intense interest, and the great European powers quickly exploited rapid technological developments in ship design, steam power, steel-making, and weaponry to build ever-more-advanced warships. At a time when Admiral Porter was ordering

American ships to use only sail and threatening to charge captains personally for the coal if they ran their engines, the British were abandoning sail for coal and building steam-driven armored ships, like *Dreadnought* in 1875, that were clearly the direct grandparents of the great battleships of the twentieth century, including the last *Missouri*. These new British battleships carried their big guns in turrets in front of and behind their bridges and smokestacks and were designed to destroy other battleships in the open seas anywhere in the world.

Over the next decades European nations spent hundreds of millions of dollars building even more powerful battleships and increasing their war fleets. Europe competed not only for the strongest fleets, but for the most foreign colonies and naval bases in Africa, Asia, and the Pacific Ocean. Few Americans were willing to pay to join the race for more modern warships and bigger fleets. Indeed, when Americans thought there might be war with Spain in 1873 over brutal Spanish treatment of their Cuban colony, Admiral Porter said "it would be much better to have no navy at all than one like the present," which was much weaker than the Spanish fleet. As late as 1889 the U.S. Navy ranked twelfth in the world in size, weaker than the navies of such countries as Turkey, China, and Austria-Hungary.

Still Americans were concerned about European naval advances and imperial competition for colonies. Since the Monroe Doctrine of 1823, America had warned European states to leave Central and South America alone to develop free democracies. Americans were especially angered by Spain's treatment of Cuba, and the ruthless suppression of rebels. At the same time, American sailors saw that modern coal-burning battle fleets required coaling stations and repair bases at strategic locations like Hawaii. Americans also saw that to defend the country's Atlantic and Pacific coasts, a canal through Central America that would allow the fleet to move quickly to counter a Spanish, or later a

Japanese, threat would be very desirable. Indeed, by the mid-1890s, Americans were growing increasingly worried about Japan. Many Americans feared waves of Japanese immigrants, and in 1897 American businessmen who had overthrown the Hawaiian royal family deported one thousand Japanese. In response to this insult, the Japanese sent a threatening cruiser to Hawaii. The new assistant secretary of the navy, Teddy Roosevelt, wanted to annex Hawaii to keep the islands from the Japanese and to serve as a base to protect Panama and the American West Coast.

The crisis came not from Japan, though, but from Spain. Both Cuban and Filipino guerrillas were battling Spanish colonial authorities, and in January 1898 the navy sent the small, new, but already obsolete 6,500-ton second-class battleship *Maine* to Havana harbor to discourage Spanish-led anti-American riots. On February, 15, 1898, a terrible explosion destroyed *Maine* and killed 260 of her crew. To this day, the exact cause of the explosion is unknown, but it appears likely that the ship was destroyed by an accidental fire in the coal supply that set off ammunition. American newspapers and many citizens blamed Spanish sabotage, and Congress immediately appropriated $50 million to expand the navy.

The United States government demanded Cuban independence, called for 125,000 volunteers, and declared a blockade of Cuba. To supplement the small American fleet, the navy took over private merchant ships, including a 15,000-ton Atlantic passenger liner called *St. Louis*. She had been built in Philadelphia in 1894, the same year that the original naval sloop *St. Louis* was lent to the Pennsylvania Naval Militia in Philadelphia as a training ship. *St. Louis* had been in transatlantic service for three years when the navy armed her with 12 guns and commissioned her a U.S. Navy auxiliary cruiser. With a speed of 23 miles per hour she was faster than the most modern battleships. On April 30, 1898, commanded by Captain Casper Goodrich and with a crew of 27 officers and 350 men, *St Louis* sailed from New York to join the American fleet in the Caribbean.

By the time *St. Louis* arrived off Spanish Puerto Rico in the second week of May, Captain George Dewey had already won a great naval victory on the other side of the world. Thirty years after serving aboard the old *Mississippi* at Port Hudson, Louisiana, he had supervised the sea trials of the navy's newest and most powerful battleships. On May 1, 1898, in an astonishing victory, Dewey's squadron of five cruisers destroyed the Spanish Asian fleet at Manila Bay. The forts and city of Manila surrendered to the navy, and the United States soon won the Philippine Islands as part of America's new empire. Against the destruction of ten Spanish ships and the loss of almost four hundred killed or wounded, Dewey's fleet did not lose a single man.

With Dewey's great Pacific victory, the navy now prepared to meet another Spanish fleet steaming across the Atlantic toward Cuba and Puerto Rico. As the American fleet blockaded Cuba and waited for the Spaniards to appear, Captain Goodrich's *St. Louis* played an important role in helping to isolate Spanish defenders on the Caribbean islands. Underwater telegraph cables had first been laid before the Civil War, and by the end of the nineteenth century many Caribbean islands were connected by such cables. *St. Louis* was fitted with heavy drag lines to snag and cut Spanish undersea cables, and on May 13, 1898, cut the telegraph line connecting San Juan, Puerto Rico with St. Thomas in the Danish Virgin Islands. A week later *St. Louis* exchanged fire with the forts guarding Santiago de Cuba, and cut the cable between this port and Jamaica. The next day the arriving Spanish fleet slipped unnoticed past the patrolling American fleet and reached the safety of the harbor of Santiago de Cuba. *St. Louis* next cut the Guantánamo Bay—Haiti and Cienfuegos cables to completely isolate Cuba. The Spanish fleet was safe from the blockading American battleships but cut off from Spain.

Liner *St. Louis* at the
blockade of Cuba.
(Naval Historical Center)

In June *St. Louis* helped bombard the fortifications at
Guantánamo Bay, captured a Spanish merchant ship, and
intercepted two British freighters sailing to Cuba. With
his ships threatened by advancing American and Cuban
troops, the Spanish admiral decided to try to break through
the American blockading force on July 3, 1898. The American warships, whose engineers and coaling crews worked
feverishly in terrible heat to feed their furnaces, quickly
caught and overwhelmed the Spanish ships. Their admiral
ran his flagship aground on the Cuban coast and swam
ashore with most of his sailors. As at Manila Bay, the entire
Spanish fleet and hundreds of Spanish sailors were lost.
Only one American was killed. Thirty-five years after an
earlier *St. Louis* and the other Eads City ironclads helped
Grant and Sherman capture Vicksburg, Rear Admiral

William Sampson telegraphed to Washington: "the fleet . . . offers the nation, as a Fourth of July present, the whole [Spanish] fleet."

The new auxiliary cruiser *St. Louis* was one of several smaller navy ships in the blockading squadron watching as the powerful new American battlefleet destroyed the outmatched Spanish cruisers. As a former passenger liner, she transported hundreds of prisoners of war, including their admiral, to Plymouth, New Hampshire. The Battle of Santiago de Cuba effectively ended the Spanish-American War. In September, *St. Louis* was returned to her civilian owner and resumed passenger service between New York and Liverpool, England, until she was again required for navy service in World War I.

The United States was delighted at the great victories won by the American navy, and many felt that powerful armored battleships and cruisers armed with heavy long-range guns were the decisive modern weapons of ocean warfare. As part of the American war fever following the destruction of *Maine* in Havana harbor, Congress had approved the construction of three new 12,000-ton battle-ships to add to the ten already in the fleet or under con-struction. Three days after Dewey's victory in Manila Bay, Congress gave final authorization for these three *Maine* class "sea-going coast-line" battleships—*Maine, Missouri,* and *Ohio.* Powered by 16,000 horsepower coal-fired recip-rocating engines that gave them a top speed of 20 miles per hour and a range of 4,900 miles, they were the first American battleships protected by new high-strength 12-inch armor. *Missouri* and *Ohio* were also the first American battleships equipped with radios. In two electrically pow-ered turrets they carried four 12-inch main guns built in the Washington Navy Yard gun factory. With very power-ful new smokeless gunpowder designed to ease the gun-smoke that had almost caused American warships to ram each other during the confused battle of Santiago de Cuba,

The third *Missouri* awash and steaming at high speed.
(Naval Historical Center)

the main guns could fire 870-pound shells 15,000 yards, or almost 8 miles. They also carried sixteen 6-inch rapid fire guns for defense against fast torpedo boats and two torpedo tubes to attack enemy battleships. The ships were 393 feet long and 72 feet wide—twice the size of Eads's Civil War gunboats but only a bit bigger than British warships like *Dreadnought* of a quarter-century earlier. Because Congress intended them for coastal defense rather than worldwide all-weather service, these early American battleships were as heavily armed and armored as their European counterparts, but they tended to be somewhat smaller and lower in the water, with less coal storage. This made them less suited to long cruises or rough seas and stormy weather. Like all early American battleships they suffered from poor ventilation, which made them almost unbearable in hot weather. They were also so wet in heavy seas that many of their smaller guns and their torpedos could not be used because of flooding.

The three sister ships were built in different private shipyards and cost about five million dollars each. *Missouri* was built by Newport News Shipbuilding in Virginia. Her keel was laid in February 1900, she was launched in December 1901, and commissioned two years later on December 1, 1903. She carried a crew of forty officers and over five hundred men, and one of her young midshipmen was William F. Halsey Jr., who would later gain fame as Admiral "Bull" Halsey in World War II. Members of the Missouri Daughters of the American Revolution knitted clothing for *Missouri*'s crew.

In February 1904 *Missouri* left Hampton Roads for Guantánamo to join the Atlantic Fleet. On April 13, while practicing with her main guns off Pensacola, Florida, *Missouri* suffered a terrible accident in her rear turret. Hot gases ignited 340 pounds of powder in the turret and 720 pounds in the shell-handling room below. While the powder did not explode, it burned and suffocated over thirty crewmen in the turret and handling room. The turret was quickly flooded to put out the fire before it reached the main magazine and destroyed the ship. As the deadly powder fumes cleared, a team of sailors went into the magazine to inspect the damage. Three of them discovered that the twelve-inch magazine, filled with one thousand pounds of powder, was still afire. Gunner's mate Mons Monssen, a native of Norway, threw water on the fire with his hands. Gunner Charles S. Schepke stayed with Monssen while acting gunner Robert E. Cox fetched a hose with which they extinguished the fire and saved the ship. The three were awarded Medals of Honor for their heroism.

Missouri's dead were given a huge military funeral, and the accident caused a long and bitter debate about whether U.S. Navy firing procedures, ammunition handling, and turret design were safer against accident or enemy shellfire than modern foreign battleships.

Following repairs, *Missouri* joined other Atlantic Fleet ships in a visit to the Mediterranean, home of one of the British Royal Navy's strongest fleets. In October 1905 her squadron escorted a British squadron back to New York. During 1906 *Missouri* won marksmanship awards for her main twelve-inch guns, six-inch guns, and torpedoes. By August 1906, according to a navy newsletter, "*Missouri* has been making a record . . . this year . . . nothing short of distinguish[ed]. . . . First in target practice of the Atlantic Fleet, first in the football games, first in the rifle practice, first in the pulling races."

In January 1907 *Missouri* landed sailors and marines in Kingston, Jamaica, to help the residents following an earthquake and fire. The local British governor was embarrassed by the absence of British ships and was offended that American ships began humanitarian action without first saluting the British flag. He resigned as governor after his demand that the U.S. Navy withdraw caused an international scandal, but his hurt feelings contributed to a cool reception for *Missouri* and the rest of the fleet when they next visited Jamaica on their around-the-world cruise at the end of the year.

Great Britain had been the greatest naval power in the world for over a hundred years, but at the beginning of the twentieth century she was challenged by a growing American navy and by new regional naval powers Germany and Japan. Britain viewed Germany as the more serious threat, but many Americans, especially those in the West, were prejudiced against Asians. Although Chinese laborers had helped build the transcontinental railroad forty years earlier, California had passed anti-Chinese laws. American businessmen in Hawaii had angered Japan in 1897 by expelling Japanese laborers, and in 1906 California's anti-Asian policies again angered and insulted Japanese leaders.

In April 1906, San Francisco was struck by an earthquake and a fire that killed thousands and left over half of the city's 400,000 residents homeless. Many of San Francisco's 74 schools were also destroyed, and in October the San

Francisco school board forbade Asian children to attend school with American children. There were also anti-Japanese attacks and riots and wild newspaper stories claiming that the Japanese navy would attack California without warning. Japan protested the treatment of its citizens, and a Japanese newspaper urged: "Stand up, Japanese nation! Our countrymen have been humiliated. . . . Our poor boys and girls have been expelled from the public schools by the rascals of the United States, cruel and merciless like devils. . . . Why do we not insist on sending ships?"

The Japanese reached a "gentlemen's agreement" with President Teddy Roosevelt under which Japan agreed not to allow any further labor migration to America if the U.S. agreed not to formally exclude Japanese workers. This humiliating agreement was strained by further anti-Japanese riots in San Francisco, and war hysteria arose in popular newspapers in both countries. Roosevelt was denounced in the *San Francisco Chronicle:* "Our feeling is not against Japan, but against an unpatriotic president who unites with aliens to break down the civilization of his own countrymen." The president expressed his anger at the "infernal fools in California" who "insult the Japanese recklessly" and the

> worse than criminal stupidity of the San Francisco mob, the San Francisco press, and . . . the *New York Herald.* I do not believe we will have war, but it is no fault of the . . . [tabloid] press if we do not have it. The Japanese seem to have about the same proportion of prize . . . [super-nationalist] fools that we have.

The crisis eased, but heightened public attention to America's vulnerable Pacific coast gave Roosevelt the opportunity to make a bold military and diplomatic gesture to underline United States world status and naval power. From its beginnings as a slender string of colonies hugging the Atlantic coast, America had focused its attention on the European powers. Even as the United States expanded to reach across the continent, its diplomatic and military efforts remained attuned to European rivals and threats; however, it could not ignore the possibility of attack from the west. In order to connect the two coasts of the country more quickly, and avoid the long, dangerous voyage around Cape Horn at the bottom of South America, a railroad was built through Panama in the 1850s to shorten the trip from Atlantic to Pacific. In the 1880s the French, after building the Suez Canal to connect the Mediterranean Sea and the Indian Ocean, tried unsuccessfully to cut a canal through Panama. Since 1903, when America had encouraged Panama to revolt and declare independence from Colombia, the United States had been spending hundreds of millions of dollars and using tens of thousands of workers to cut a new Panama canal for commercial and military purposes.

The Japanese war scare made many Americans think that the West Coast might need more protection against enemy attack and that the navy should make plans to move the new fleet into the Pacific if danger threatened. Roosevelt was unwilling to divide his battleships between Atlantic and Pacific bases, and with the Panama Canal unfinished, he decided to send the whole fleet on a "training" cruise to the Pacific. He wanted to show Japan that America could mass military strength in the Pacific if necessary, to encourage popular support and funding for the fleet, and to emphasize the need to complete the Panama Canal.

While Californians were delighted that the fleet would visit San Francisco, easterners expressed alarm at the cost of moving the whole fleet and fear that the Atlantic coast would be left defenseless. Wild and irrational rumors flew that the German Navy might suddenly attack America or that the Japanese might try to sabotage the fleet.

Roosevelt's plan was incredibly ambitious. No navy had ever succeeded in such a complicated voyage. Would the engines and machinery hold up? Would the "coastal defense" battleships be able to withstand wild ocean storms? Would the navy be able to supply the 90 tons of coal that each battleship would consume every day—1,500 tons a day for the entire fleet? Would the officers and crews be up to the challenges of such a long journey? And would the trip leave ships and crews so worn out that they would take months to recover?

At first, Roosevelt hid the full extent of his plans, perhaps fearing that the fleet might not be able to face the challenge before them. Atlantic Fleet commander in chief, Rear Admiral Robley D. "Fighting Bob" Evans, ordered his sixteen battleships, from the seven-year-old 11,000 ton *Kearsarge* and *Kentucky* to the brand-new 16,000 ton *Virginia, Connecticut*, and *Vermont* class ships, to prepare for a long cruise and assemble in early December 1907 in Hampton Roads, Virginia. The navy planned five coaling stops all around South America, and chartered a fleet of foreign-owned coal ships to help supply the 125,000 tons of coal that the fleet was expected to burn during the voyage to California.

Thousands of Americans flocked to Norfolk and Hampton, Virginia, to see the fleet off. Not all of the 13,000 sailors in the fleet were able to celebrate the adventure, however. A number of Japanese had joined the navy as cooks and officers' servants. Some naval officers feared that these crewmen might remain loyal to Japan and try to sabotage their ships if they ever faced the Japanese navy. Seventy-two Japanese were therefore removed from the ships just before departure. One was so upset at being suspected of disloyalty that he tried to drown himself.

After weeks of storm and blizzard, Monday, December 16, 1907, was a clear bright day. The sixteen battleships, painted gleaming white, their rigging covered with flags,

Great White Fleet departing from Norfolk.
(Naval Historical Center)

were reviewed by President Roosevelt, who exclaimed "Did you ever see such a fleet! Isn't it magnificent?" Admiral Evans had assured Americans "you will not be disappointed in the fleet, whether it proves a feast, a frolic, or a fight," and Roosevelt clearly agreed. He summoned the admirals and captains for a last farewell and shook hands with them all, including Captain Greenlief Merriam of *Missouri.* The ships offered many twenty-one gun salutes; a band played "The Star-Spangled Banner" and other patriotic and popular tunes; finally, the presidential yacht led the fleet in a column almost four miles long out into the Atlantic Ocean. As the ships headed south, newspapers all over the world offered opinions on the cruise. The *Berliner Tageblatt* called it "the greatest naval experiment ever undertaken by any nation in time of peace," and a Japanese newspaper predicted "should the American fleet visit . . . it will be given a . . . reception worthy of the special friendship between Japan and the United States."

Admiral Evans immediately began the hard work of turning the sixteen ships' raw crews of inexperienced recruits and new captains into a disciplined fleet. The battleships were formed into four divisions, with the newest ship, *Minnesota*, and the older sister ships *Maine*, *Missouri*, and *Ohio* in the third division under Rear Admiral Charles Thomas. The ships sailed in close formation, each one following at four hundred yards from the one in front, a feat demanding great skill and attention from officers, engineers, and crews to keep accurate speed and position as the fleet maneuvered. On the first night at sea, Admiral Evans tried to ease the curiosity of officers and men in a radio message to the fleet announcing that after their visit to San Francisco, they would return home by way of the Suez Canal—in other words, by steaming west across the Pacific, Indian, and Atlantic Oceans and around the world. The radio message was intended only for the fleet but was heard ashore, and this sensational news was published in American newspapers. President Roosevelt immediately denied the newspaper reports, still not confident that the ships and men could succeed in such a long journey.

Indeed, as the fleet sailed down the East Coast, some ships suffered mechanical breakdowns, and "children's diseases" like mumps, scarlet fever, chicken pox, as well as more serious illnesses, began to strike the crews of the crowded ships. *Missouri* reported a case of typhoid fever and stopped in Puerto Rico to drop off the sailor before he infected the whole crew. *Alabama* lost a man to spinal meningitis, and the fleet paused while he was buried at sea.

Two days before Christmas, after steaming 1,800 miles, the fleet reached Port of Spain, Trinidad, for its first coaling stop. Admiral Evans, who had been crippled during the Civil War, had to be supported by two junior officers as he and his admirals went ashore to a polite but cool British reception. Perhaps they were still unhappy about the incident involving *Missouri* in January or embarrassed at the arrival of the Great White Fleet of 16 gleaming American battleships when the proud royal navy did not have a single warship in port. The British governor discouraged local businessmen from holding a ball in honor of the visitors, and when the British military invited 250 American officers to a reception, only a handful of senior officers showed up. Still, many sailors went ashore to play baseball, shop, and mail thousands of postcards home, and they behaved so well that in the end the British governor congratulated Admiral Evans on their conduct and discipline.

The main purpose of the visit, of course, was to refuel the ships for the long voyage to South America. Loading the ships with coal was the dirtiest, most unpleasant duty in the early steam navy, and all officers and men wore their oldest clothes for this job. The ships' bands played ragtime music to encourage the men, and they worked during the entire visit except on Christmas day. Finally the sailors scrubbed off all the black coal dust that covered the ships and themselves. This dirty, backbreaking job would be repeated at every port during the next fifteen months as they sailed around the world.

The White Fleet left port on December 29, minus 60 sailors who had deserted rather than continue the journey. According to records, *Missouri* was a relatively unhappy ship, losing 94 men in 1907. Only three battleships lost more. In 1908 only two ships lost more, with *Missouri* suffering 108 desertions. The ships celebrated New Year 1908 at sea with homemade costumes and music, but the biggest celebration was several days later when the fleet

first day hatch
after coaling
Photo by
Surgent.

Sailors of the Great
White Fleet coaling.
(Naval Historical
Center)

crossed the equator and entered the southern hemisphere. For 12,000 of the 14,000 members of the fleet this was their first crossing, and King Neptune and his court visited every ship to initiate his new subjects by shaving their heads, painting their faces with flour and molasses, and dunking them in water tanks.

Such celebrations kept up the sailors' morale and pride, but Evans and his officers soon received an unpleasant surprise. They had underestimated the distance between Trinidad and Rio de Janeiro, Brazil—some 3,400 miles— by at least 400 miles. The admirals feared that some of the older or less efficient ships might run out of coal, and

Admiral Thomas wrote "it would be awful if we were compelled to tow these ships into port." Evans ordered strict economy, including slower speed, less attention to tight formation, and even restrictions on electric lighting and freshwater bathing. The fleet was further slowed by a mistaken report from *Missouri* that a sailor had fallen overboard.

Fortunately, *Missouri* had not lost a crewman, and the coal held out. The fleet reached Rio on January 12, 1908, to an enthusiastic welcome by South America's biggest and most powerful country. The senior officers immediately began a heavy schedule of official diplomatic ceremonies, although Admiral William Emory complained of having to wear his heavy wool formal uniform in the tropical summer: "the good Lord never afflicted such misery on a human being as He did upon me." Rio welcomed the American sailors, and despite a few brawls and stabbings, a Brazilian newspaper praised the "youthful and orderly" sailors. The sailors were of course less happy to again have to coal the ships for the 2,000-mile run down to the Strait of Magellan at the tip of South America.

The fleet and their Brazilian hosts had received warnings from around the world that the Japanese or Germans, or even European anarchists, might attack the ships with mines or try to sabotage the coal supplies. Although the stories proved groundless, the Japanese navy took the remarkable step of giving the American embassy in Tokyo daily reports of the location of Japanese warships. While the Brazilians expressed great friendship for America, the Americans did not forget that they had just ordered three powerful new British "dreadnought" battleships—stronger, faster, and more deadly than any of the American White Fleet. The fleet intelligence officers thus made careful note of Brazilian defenses, although one junior officer warned his mother: "please don't tell anyone that officers . . . do such things because some people might think it wasn't . . . courteous." The fleet left Rio on January 22, and Admiral Evans established a competition among the ships with prizes and rewards for the ship that could save the most coal and steam most economically.

The officers and men responded so enthusiastically to this challenge that the fleet managed to cut its coal consumption by 20 percent during the rest of the cruise. During the passage down the Atlantic coast of South America, the crews practiced with advanced new technology. First, they finished installing telephone fire-control systems so the officers could more accurately direct the aim of the ships' big guns. Although the American navy had won great victories at Manila Bay and Santiago de Cuba, gunnery officers discovered that only one or two shells of every hundred fired hit the enemy ships. Modern navies, including the American fleet, invested much effort and thought in new scientific technology to improve the power and accuracy of weapons. The White Fleet was also equipped with radios so the admirals could direct all their ships, no matter the weather or distance between them. During the 2,300-mile journey to the Atlantic end of the Strait of Magellan, the admirals and captains practiced controlling and maneuvering their battleships using this new "wireless" communication tool.

The navy's torpedo squadron escorted the battleships as they navigated the dangerous final 140 miles to the Pacific Ocean. The strait was made dangerous by its many small islands and frequent fog, but the torpedo boats were there to guard against such imagined enemies as German or Japanese mines or submarines that fearful Americans— encouraged by hysterical newspaper editorials—thought might be lurking in ambush.

The fleet reached the Pacific safely, and on Valentine's Day 1908 it made a brief but spectacular visit to Valparaiso harbor where the ships put on "the most magnificent marine pageant ever seen in the Pacific Ocean, and probably in the whole world." Seventeen years earlier Captain Robley Evans in command of *Yorktown* had threatened to shell Valparaiso during confrontation between the Chilean and American navies, but this time the fleet made a great loop through the harbor, flying Chilean flags and firing twenty-one-gun salutes to Chilean president Pedro Montt. Admiral Thomas proudly called the performance the most "perfect exhibition of Marine Efficiency, power, and drill . . . in the World's history."

Four days later the fleet arrived in Callao, Peru, and in honor of the visit President Jose Pardo declared George Washington's birthday a national holiday. The Peruvians staged a grand bullfight to entertain three thousand American sailors, but many were so appalled by the cruelty of the sport that they cheered for the bulls and left the stadium early.

As the fleet reached Mexico, Rear Admiral Evans radioed the Navy Department to announce the arrival of the fleet, and the whole country celebrated the navy's remarkable success in moving the fleet from the Atlantic to the Pacific coasts. Admiral Thomas boasted that the fleet had arrived in better condition than when it had left Norfolk four months earlier. The crews were well trained and strong, the officers were skilled, and the engineers had learned to maintain and repair the ships' engines and machinery themselves without having to depend on ship-yard repair shops. President Roosevelt was so delighted at the condition of the fleet that he allowed the navy to officially announce that it would return home across the Pacific and through the Suez Canal—something he had denied when the fleet left Norfolk.

When the Great White Fleet finally reached the coast of California on April 14, 1908, the progress of the ships from San Diego to San Francisco turned into one huge celebration. San Diego set bonfires on the beaches, and young women bore bouquets of flowers out to sea to spread around the battleships. As the ships steamed toward Los Angeles, huge crowds came to the shore to watch them pass, and tens of thousands camped overnight on beaches in San Pedro, Long Beach, and Santa Monica to await their arrival. To allow more people to see the ships, the divisions anchored at different ports. *Missouri* and her Third Division sisters *Minnesota, Ohio,* and *Maine* went to Santa Monica. The Los Angeles visit was not altogether happy. Because Easter Sunday fell during the visit, local churches tried to get the city to close the saloons during the entire time the ships were in port. One local leader wrote commander Admiral Thomas, "It will certainly be a proud day when [we can say of the navy] not a man of them is known to drink, on duty or off."

Even worse happened in Santa Barbara. A number of wives had traveled across the country for brief visits with their sailor husbands. Santa Barbara restaurants and hotels raised their prices so high and treated the sailors so badly that hundreds of them rioted, breaking windows and forcing the owners to flee.

As might be expected, the welcome in San Francisco was much warmer, since that city's anti-Japanese school policies had inspired the cruise in the first place. Local citizens raised thousands of dollars to entertain the fleet, with the Japanese community giving one of the largest contributions. More than a half million people filled San Francisco, Oakland, and the hills of Marin County to await the fleet.

On May 6, to the cheers of the vast crowd, Admiral Evans led the combined fleet through the Golden Gate and paraded his forty-six warships down San Francisco Bay and back up to the city. One spectator wrote "our hearts beat high with pride in our own country, and in the sure protection of its invincible strength."

As a highlight of the visit 7,500 sailors and marines marched through the city in the largest military parade ever held on the West Coast. Admiral Evans was given a

Missouri bear cub:
Seattle's gift to the
Great White Fleet.
(Naval Historical Center)

jeweled sword by the people of San Francisco, and the sailors and officers were entertained with parties and tours. After the fleet left San Francisco it made a brief visit to Washington, where 400,000 people flocked to the small city of Seattle in Puget Sound to see it and watch yet another "monster parade." The people of Seattle gave each battleship a bear cub as a mascot to add to the zoo that each ship already carried. The sailors loved pet animals, and pigs, goats, monkeys, cats, dogs, and parrots filled the ships. The fleet had even carried a full-grown tiger until he jumped overboard into the Strait of Magellan and was lost.

Freshly painted, refueled, and repaired, the Great White Fleet returned to San Francisco in early July to head west toward Asia. Captain Merriam was replaced as *Missouri*'s captain by Commander Robert Doyle, who would bring

her back home. Many Californians wanted the Atlantic
Fleet to remain permanently, and the city of San Diego
appealed to President Roosevelt to leave the fleet to defend
the Pacific coast. Roosevelt, however, sent the fleet a message of praise and farewell: " Heartiest good wishes . . .
the American people can trust the skilled efficiency and
devotion to duty of the Fleet. . . . You have . . . the honor of
the United States in your keeping and no . . . men in the
world enjoy . . . a greater privilege or carry a heavier
responsibility."

The new American colony of Hawaii declared the arrival
of the fleet a holiday, and thousands of people waited on
Diamond Head to see the ships appear. The admiral
detoured past the island of Molokai so the inhabitants of
the leper colony there could see the parade of ships and
then arrived in Honolulu to the welcome of a fleet of decorated passenger steamers. Although the United States
had annexed the remote and exotic Hawaiian Islands fifteen years earlier, in part as a naval base, the islands were
still so underdeveloped that only one battleship at a time
could coal in Honolulu harbor, and *Missouri* and the rest of
the Third Division had to refuel at Lahaina on Maui. Congress had just authorized a million dollars to develop Pearl
Harbor outside Honolulu as the fleet's main Pacific base,
and Rear Admiral Seaton Schroeder and all his officers
visited the site. Among those inspecting the harbor were
Ensigns Harold Stark, Husband Kimmel, and William
Halsey. Thirty-three years later, Kimmel would be commander of the Pacific Fleet at Pearl Harbor, when the
Japanese attacked on December 7, 1941. Halsey, in command of an aircraft carrier, would be away from Pearl, and
his ship would escape the general destruction. Stark would
be chief of naval operations in Washington.

Most Hawaiians welcomed the American sailors with tra-
ditional warmth and hospitality, showering them with leis,

but Queen Liliuokalani, who had been overthrown by American planters in 1893, refused to take part in the celebration. The sailors marveled at the beauty of the islands, the exotic appearance of the natives, and the local customs. Their letters home and newspaper reports of the visit gave most Americans their first real picture of this new American territory.

On July 22 the fleet left Honolulu for the longest leg of the trip—3,850 miles to Auckland, New Zealand. As it departed, a ship's surgeon wrote, "Honolulu never looked prettier than it did in the evening light as we sailed away . . . we saw the lights of the town for several hours . . . and as soon as it was a little dark a good many fireworks were sent up."

The first half of the voyage, from Norfolk to California, had been primarily a military exercise to demonstrate naval power and efficiency. The trip home was much more about diplomacy, with the fleet visiting Pacific countries important to America. At the same time, New Zealand and Australia sought American friendship, worried that waves of Japanese immigrants would soon outnumber "Europeans." They also feared the growing power of the Japanese navy and felt they could no longer depend upon the British navy's small Pacific Squadron. The new fleet commander, Rear Admiral Charles S. Sperry, who had replaced the ailing Admiral Evans in California, did not want to play on "yellow peril" fears. During his visit to New Zealand and Australia, he thus carefully spoke only of Anglo-American friendship and common commercial interests.

Sperry's cautious diplomatic language did not dampen the warm welcome the fleet received when it arrived in Auckland on August 9 after more than two weeks at sea. Fully 10 percent of New Zealand's population—100,000 people—turned out to greet it, and the whole city was decorated with flags and pictures of President Roosevelt and

King Edward VII. During their week in Auckland, the
sailors were enthusiastically entertained with parties,
tours, and horse races. American and British sailors
danced in the streets with local citizens, and the Americans
bought toys and native Maori crafts and mailed home over
40,000 postcards. As part of the ceremonies honoring the
fleet, sixteen oak trees were planted in Albert Park, one
named for *Missouri* and the others for her sisters in the
fleet. The Americans called New Zealanders the "healthi-
est, happiest, most prosperous" people in the world and
New Zealanders were equally delighted with their visitors. Local newspapers proclaimed the two countries
bound by "ties of blood, of religion, of origin, of ideals, of
aspirations." The country also saw the visit, however, as a
demonstration "against Oriental immigration into the
White Man's Lands."

The welcome in Australia was no less warm. In Sydney
the fleet was greeted by over a half million people—more
than had celebrated the founding of the Commonwealth of
Australia. Twelve thousand British, American, and Australian servicemen marched in the largest military parade
in Australian history. Then the southern winter turned
cold, and by the end of the visit, an officer joked that "the
visitor was overtired, the shows overlong, the skies over-
cast, and the winds overcold."

Worn out from their reception in Sydney, the crews were
not looking forward to Melbourne, where local officials
were determined to put on an even bigger party for the
Americans. Indeed, only seven sailors appeared for a dinner prepared for three thousand guests at the Exhibition
Building. A local newspaper explained the "fiasco of the
'Uneaten Dinner': when every tar . . . has a girl on his arm
it is easily understood that he does not want to leave the
lights and the crowd [to eat dinner with his shipmates.]"
At a fireworks display the next evening, there also seemed
to be few sailors: "But they were *there,* very much so. Every

The Great White Fleet visiting Sydney.
(Naval Historical Center)

rocket revealed tender scenes. Only here and there, a girl had secured the attention of a sailor boy all to herself. Most of them walked with two girls—an arm around each."

Indeed, Melbourne turned out to be the most popular liberty port on the entire cruise, and the city treated the Americans so well that many sailors were late returning to their ships because mobs of girls hugging and kissing them blocked their way back to the docks. Over 100 deserted, with one young officer writing his parents: "If I were not in the Navy I would settle here myself. For a young man of energy there is a fortune waiting." So many sailors were late that on *Georgia* 87 percent of her 850 first-class seamen were demoted in punishment.

The fleet reached the scene of Admiral Dewey's great Manila Bay victory on October 2. Upon arrival they discovered that Manila was suffering from a cholera epidemic.

All local celebrations and most shore leaves were thus cancelled, and the crews spent the whole Philippine stay coaling the ships in the blazing tropical heat and humidity. Because of the length of the voyage to Yokohama, Japan, extra coal was heaped on deck. Coaling was disrupted by a typhoon with one hundred-mile-an-hour winds on October 4, but the fleet only lost a few small boats.

The fleet left Manila on October 10, and two days later ran into a second typhoon. Even the largest modern battleships "wallowed like a herd of swine"; smaller ships were forced to slow to a crawl. *Missouri*'s decks were repeatedly swamped by huge waves, and the officers and men on her bridge were soaked by spray. Other ships lost boats, masts, and radio antenna, and three sailors were swept overboard. Two were rescued by following ships, but when *Rhode Island*, sailing at the rear of the fleet, lost a man, the crew, unable to turn or lower a rescue boat because of the storm, could only watch him "in the water looking after the ship" as they steamed away.

In spite of years of bitter tension between Americans and Japanese, Japan welcomed the Great White Fleet with warmth, hospitality, and careful preparation. A squadron of gray Japanese cruisers accompanied by six merchant ships with WELCOME painted on their black hulls met the fleet. The merchant ships were crowded with Japanese men, women, and children, all cheering and singing American patriotic songs in English. Thousands of Japanese schoolchildren had been taught to sing "The Star-Spangled Banner" and other songs. While the fleet was in Japan student volunteers acted as guides and interpreters for the American sailors. Admiral Sperry was equally careful to avoid offense, and his sailors were closely supervised to prevent any misbehavior while in Japan.

The high point of the visit was an audience with the Emperor on October 20 in Tokyo. The meeting went so well that the Emperor joined the state luncheon for the Ameri-

Japanese officers aboard *Missouri* at Yokohama.
(Naval Historical Center)

can commanders and "chatted amiably" through the whole
meal. Three days later the Japanese navy entertained the
American officers on the British-built battleship *Mikasa*,
with Japanese admirals and captains hoisting the American admirals and ambassador on their shoulders and
parading them around the decks. Next day Admiral Sperry
returned the hospitality on his flagship, *Connecticut*, but
over 3,300 Japanese guests quickly exhausted the food and
drink. In contrast to Japanese lavishness, the Americans
had only budgeted $1,300 to entertain their guests. As an
American officer wrote: "it was as sad an affair as the *Mikasa*
was beautiful. Oh my, oh my, Americans have a great deal
to learn in polite manners." The Japanese were polite, and

the whole visit was considered a great diplomatic success. President Roosevelt wrote, "My policy of constant friendliness and courtesy toward Japan, *coupled with sending the fleet around the world,* has borne good results."

Finally, on December 1, 1908, flying "homeward-bound pennants" that were two hundred feet long, the fleet left Manila for Colombo, Ceylon, and home. After a quick passage the fleet paused in Colombo to coal and marvel at the "rickshaw men, shopkeepers, tattooers, and a whole rabble of . . . people telling [us] where the most beautiful Singhalese girls could be found, very cheap."

After more than a year away from home, the crews grew increasingly excited as they steamed through the Indian Ocean toward the Red Sea and the Suez Canal. The sailors on *Illinois* began planning a ball to celebrate their return to Boston, and with their band playing, practiced waltzes on the decks. In the Red Sea the battleships were given three cheers by British soldiers on a troopship bound for India. They entered the Suez Canal in early January.

When it reached the Mediterranean, the fleet divided to allow the ships to visit more ports before they reassembled at Gibraltar for the final leg home. *Missouri* and *Ohio* were first sent to Greece, where their captains were introduced to the queen and the royal family toured *Missouri.* After coaling, the ships visited the Turkish ports of Salonika and Smyrna to show support for a new constitutional government led by the liberal "Young Turks" party. Fifty-three years earlier, the first *St. Louis* had forced the Austrian navy to surrender Hungarian revolutionary Martin Koszta in Smyrna harbor. Other battleships visited France, British Malta, the Ottoman North African port of Tripoli, and French Algiers. They also stopped in Italy and Sicily to offer assistance to victims of a massive earthquake and tidal wave that had killed some 200,000 people.

The fleet gathered at Gibraltar in late January, joining British, Russian, French, and Dutch warships at anchor.

Missouri arrived on February 1, some sixty-six years after the first American *Missouri* had burned and sunk at Gibraltar. With so many nationalities represented, the playing of national anthems and firing of salutes took over an hour. For the next week the crews loaded their ships with coal and provisions, cleaned and touched up the paint, and polished the brasswork for the trip home. Playing "God Save the King" and "Home, Sweet Home," the fleet steamed out of Gibraltar on February 9, 1909, for the journey across the Atlantic. Five days later Admiral Sperry was able to radio his position to a naval station on Fire Island, New York, some two thousand miles ahead.

The whole fleet arrived home on February 22— Washington's birthday—to a celebration of "patriotism of the best American type" and greetings by a delighted President Roosevelt. As he said in his toast to the fleet, "Not until an American fleet returns victorious from a great sea-fight will there be another such home-coming as this. We stay-at-homes drink to the men who have made us so proud of our country."

The ships returned to their East Coast homeports, where the crews were finally reunited with their families and their ships were repainted in the new standard "battleship gray." The world cruise had been a military, political, and diplomatic triumph. The fleet had proven not only the technical reliability of its ships, but also the skill, discipline, and fortitude of its officers and men. Thanks to journalists who accompanied the fleet and wrote newspaper stories read by tens of millions of readers, American and foreign audiences learned more about the strength of the American fleet and the peoples of such distant lands as Hawaii, Australia, New Zealand, and even Japan. Finally, the bold voyage ordered by Theodore Roosevelt sent a message of solidarity to Australia, New Zealand, and other British possessions, while warning Germany and Japan of America's growing military power. Ironically, though,

the White Fleet, which seemed so powerful to foreign
crowds, was obsolete before it even left Norfolk in December of 1907.

In 1904, a brilliant naval reformer, Admiral Sir John
Fisher, had become commander in chief of the British Royal
Navy. Fisher ruthlessly scrapped older battleships and
secretly planned the most powerful and revolutionary
battleship ever seen. Designed to be faster than any other
battleship, with twice as many main guns, this new *Dreadnought* made every other warship obsolete. Built with
astonishing speed in just one year, *Dreadnought* began her
sea trials in October 1906 as *Missouri* was peacefully
patrolling the Caribbean. While only 4,000 tons heavier,
Dreadnought was 130 feet longer, carried ten 12-inch guns
to *Missouri*'s four, and most important, was powered by
smooth 23,000-horsepower turbine engines rather than the
troublesome reciprocating piston engines of earlier battleships. The turbines, which could run at top speed with little maintenance, allowed *Dreadnought* to outrun any other
battleship in the world. Her huge "all big gun" battery of
twelve-inch guns was easier to aim than the mixture of big
and small caliber guns on other ships. She was thus able to
fire accurately at such long range that she could catch and
beat any other two or three battleships in any other navy.

Other navies frantically designed comparable "dread-
noughts." Germany lost a year in the naval race, and it was
only in 1910 that the United States fielded ships of comparable gunpower and speed. Five years after the triumphal
return of the Great White Fleet, therefore, naval technology
had advanced so quickly that in August 1914 none of the
White Fleet was fit to join the battle line or face modern
"superdreadnoughts."

While most naval strategists and ordinary citizens
focused on the powerful and glamorous battle fleets, the
ordinary routine business of peacetime navies was carried
out by smaller ships or "cruisers" patrolling foreign sta-

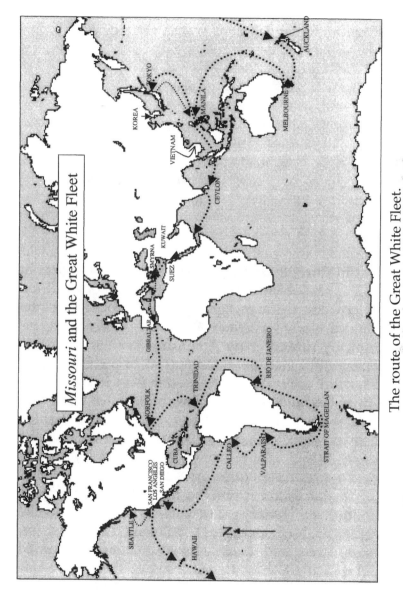

The route of the Great White Fleet.
(Courtesy Lieutenant Colonel Steve Oluic, Kent State University)

tions. The first *St. Louis* had a long and distinguished career, serving all over the world before retiring in Philadelphia. As Jackie Fisher was planning his revolutionary *Dreadnought,* another *St. Louis* was launched in Philadelphia. Some 30 feet longer than the battleship *Missouri,* she weighed 9,700 tons and had a speed of 22 knots. She carried a crew of 673 officers and men, and was armed with fourteen 6-inch guns as well as many smaller guns. This new cruiser *St. Louis* left for duty with the Pacific Fleet in May 1907, stopping at many of the same ports visited by the Great White Fleet seven months later.

St. Louis just missed the excitement of the fleet's California visits because she was visiting Hawaii and Central America as the fleet sailed westward from San Francisco. While *Missouri* returned to serve in the Atlantic, *St. Louis* spent the next few years on the West Coast. When war broke out in Europe in August 1914, the United States at first tried to remain neutral, hoping to trade with all the warring powers. German agitation and sabotage in the United States, along with their aggressive submarine campaign, quickly turned many Americans against Germany. In February 1915 Germany announced unrestricted submarine warfare around England, and in May 1915 sank the British liner *Lusitania* with great loss of life.

As the U.S. Navy made war plans, even older battleships like *Missouri* were valuable to train new sailors. In the summer of 1915 *Missouri* carried Naval Academy midshipmen on a training cruise through the Caribbean and Pacific. She and *Ohio* became the first battleships to pass through the new Panama Canal. A cadet described the tropical jungles, huge locks that swallowed the battleships, freshwater lakes, and deep cuts as the ships steamed toward the Pacific. On the transit, *Missouri* carried the U.S. Army's Canal Zone governor, his staff, and "lots of good looking [ladies]" and was cheered by U.S. Army troops as they passed. "We gave several [navy] yells and the 'Star-

Missouri and *Ohio* in the Panama Canal.
(Naval Historical Center)

Spangled Banner' . . . for it was a great occasion—the passing of the first battleship through the canal."

Missouri then went to the reserves, but cruiser *St. Louis* was assigned to Pearl Harbor. As Pearl Harbor's "station ship," she was responsible for watching the German gunboat *Geier* which had been interned in Honolulu since the outbreak of war in 1914. According to *St. Louis*'s "War Log," the *Geier* stayed in contact with German secret agents in the islands as well as with the German Pacific Squadron. In February 1917, *Geier*'s crew tried to burn their ship to damage Honolulu's port. Supported by army troops and cannon, a party from *St. Louis* boarded the burning ship and took the German crew prisoner. They discovered that the Germans had sabotaged the magazine and set the boiler afire in hopes of causing a larger and even more damaging explosion. *St. Louis* sailors towed the burning ship to a safer location and battled the blaze all day until relieved.

Within two months, *St. Louis, Missouri,* and even the Spanish-American War auxiliary passenger ship *St. Louis,* were all called to wartime duty as the United States entered World War I in April 1917. In March, the liner *St. Louis* was armed with three six-inch guns manned by twenty-six U.S. Navy sailors to protect her as she continued passenger service between New York and Liverpool, England. On May 30 in the Irish Channel she ran over a submarine that had fired a torpedo at her, and in July she exchanged cannon fire with a surfaced U-boat. *Missouri* rejoined the Atlantic Fleet as a division flagship and training ship. During the war she remained in the Chesapeake Bay area training thousands of recruits in gunnery and engineering skills.

Cruiser *St. Louis* left Pearl Harbor in early April, picked up 500 naval volunteers in San Diego to bring her up to wartime strength of 823 officers and men, and reported to Philadelphia for convoy duty. Beginning in June 1917, she escorted 7 convoys across the Atlantic, logging over 100,000 miles through the bitter North Atlantic winter storms of 1917–1918. In April 1918 passenger liner *St. Louis* was taken over by the U.S. Navy as a troop transport and renamed *Louisville*. During the war the navy's main duty was to move two million American troops and their supplies to France, and when the war ended on November 11, 1918, its happy duty was to bring the boys home.

Even *Missouri* was pressed into this service, making four round trips to Brest, France, to bring 3,278 soldiers back to America. *St. Louis* made seven trips, bringing home 8,400 soldiers, and *Louisville* made six trips ferrying soldiers. In September 1919 *Louisville* was returned to her civilian owners, who changed her name back to *St. Louis*. She caught fire in January 1920 while being reconditioned for passenger service and was so badly damaged that she was scrapped.

World War I cruiser *St. Louis* in warpaint.
(Naval Historical Center)

Cruiser *St. Louis,* now designated CA-18, was assigned to the European Squadron and in October 1920 reported to Constantinople, Turkey, where the first *St. Louis* had patrolled seventy years earlier. War and revolution still troubled the eastern Mediterranean, and *St. Louis* went to Yalta and Sevastopol to pick up refugees fleeing the Russian civil war. Revolution also broke out in Turkey, and sailors from *St. Louis* helped distribute food and other humanitarian aid to Russian and Turkish refugees in Constantinople. She returned to Philadelphia and was decommissioned in March 1922. *Missouri* was also decommissioned in Philadelphia.

At the end of the terrible World War, many people shared President Woodrow Wilson's dream that future wars could be avoided through international cooperation. To reduce the fleets to the size agreed to in postwar treaties, countries scrapped many of their older battleships. Among these ships were *Missouri* and many of her sisters from the Great White Fleet.

CHAPTER FOUR

Another *St. Louis* and the Last *Missouri*

The Second World War

While many warships from the First World War were scrapped, three of *Missouri*'s White Fleet sisters suffered a more modern fate. *Alabama, Virginia,* and *New Jersey* were all destroyed by experimental aerial bombing, with *Virginia* and *New Jersey* being sunk by General Billy Mitchell's army bombers in September 1923. Mitchell argued that modern airplanes made battleships obsolete, and the American, British, and Japanese navies converted some half-finished battleships and battlecruisers into aircraft carriers. America's first two big, fast aircraft carriers, *Lexington* and *Saratoga*, joined the fleet in 1927. They carried seventy-five planes each and were ten knots faster, and just as heavy, as the last World War I–era battleship.

In the years after the Great War, both Japanese and American naval thinkers believed that their battle plans should be designed to fight each other for control of the Pacific Ocean. The "gun club" of battleship admirals still believed that battleships were the ultimate weapon of naval superiority, and in 1924, the chief of naval operations, Admiral Edward Eberle, predicted "the battleship of the future . . . will not be subject to fatal damage from the air." In 1932, however, *Saratoga* and *Lexington*, with 152 planes, surprised Pearl Harbor with a dawn raid that would have devastated the naval base.

In the 1930s, the Great Depression threw millions out of work, and in Germany and Japan nationalists and militarists played on the people's poverty and anger and built up their armies and navies to support their imperial ambitions. In 1936 the U.S. Navy had only 19 light cruisers with 6-inch guns, but President Franklin Roosevelt's National Industrial Recovery Act jobs program included money for new light cruisers.

These new cruisers were actually almost as heavy as the Great White Fleet's *Missouri*, weighing 10,000 tons and carrying main batteries of fifteen 6-inch guns in 5 triple turrets. They were powerful enough to fight Japanese heavy cruisers. Six hundred feet long, they had a top speed of 37 miles per hour thanks to 100,000-horsepower steam turbines, could steam 7,800 miles, and carried wartime crews of 1,200 men. They were the first light cruisers to carry hangars for scout seaplanes and had two catapults to launch the planes. Each ship cost some $18 million. In December 1936 work began at Newport News shipyard on a new *St. Louis*, CL-49. Commissioned in May 1939, *St. Louis* was initially stationed in Norfolk, with a native of St. Louis, Captain Charles H. Morrison, as commander.

When Germany invaded Poland on September 1, 1939, President Roosevelt declared a "limited emergency" and raised the number of sailors in the navy to 191,000. In October *St. Louis* joined the American "neutrality patrol" watching the Atlantic and Caribbean from Newfoundland to Trinidad and guarding British convoys against Germany's small and unprepared U-boat fleet.

After the fall of France in the spring of 1940 Congress voted four billion dollars to build a two-ocean navy. Navy planners had designs ready for powerful new classes of battleships, cruisers, destroyers, and aircraft carriers. But as Admiral Harold Stark, Chief of Naval Operations, pointed out, "dollars cannot buy yesterday," and new ships took years to build. In August 1940, one of President Roosevelt's advisors warned "it is as clear as anything on this earth that the United States will not *go* to war, but it is equally clear that war is *coming* to [America]." American naval commanders focused on the battle of the Atlantic, and in September and October, *St. Louis* carried a team of inspectors on a two-month visit to possible naval and air bases from Newfoundland to Bermuda, the Bahamas, Jamaica, St. Lucia, Antigua, Trinidad, and British Guiana (now Belize) on the coast of South America.

As the war came closer to America, *St. Louis* moved to the Pacific Ocean, where she patrolled around the Hawaiian Islands. On December 1, 1941, as Japan's six largest aircraft carriers steamed toward Pearl Harbor, the Japanese combined fleet was more powerful and better trained than the U.S. Pacific Fleet. Japan had ten battleships to America's nine World War I–vintage ships—many of them "old enough to vote." Eight U.S. battleships were at Pearl Harbor. To Japan's ten aircraft carriers, the Pacific Fleet had only three. Fortunately, all three were away from Pearl. Rear Admiral William "Bull" Halsey was with *Enterprise* carrying fighter planes to Wake Island. Japan had 18 heavy and 17 light cruisers, while the United States had 13 heavies and 11 light cruisers—a number of them away from Pearl with the carriers or on patrol.

When the Japanese struck Pearl Harbor on Sunday morning, December 7, they found eight battleships, two heavy cruisers, six light cruisers, and twenty-nine destroyers lying in the harbor with cold boilers and empty guns. Many officers and men were on shore leave, and those aboard ship were beginning another quiet peacetime Sunday morning. Two of *St. Louis*'s boilers were disassembled, and workers had cut a four-foot hole in the side of the ship to make repairs easier. According to Captain George Rood's report, his crew immediately opened fire on the first wave of attacking torpedo bombers. Men at the larger five-inch turrets also quickly began shooting at high-alti-

Lieutenant Commander
Samuel Glenn Fuqua:
hero of *Arizona*.
(Naval Historical Center)

tude bombers. Because the electrical system was under repair, the gunners had to load and fire by hand. The engineers lit the boilers, sealed the hole in the ship's side, and began trying to get under way to escape the death trap of Pearl Harbor.

The Japanese concentrated their fire on the helpless battleships. *Arizona* was struck by aerial bombs, which exploded her magazine and killed her captain and admiral. One of *Arizona's* officers, Lieutenant Commander Samuel Fuqua of Laddonia, Missouri, was stunned by the explosion of a Japanese bomb. When he regained consciousness he led the crew in fighting fires and rescuing wounded shipmates in the face of continued enemy attacks. He rallied the crew:

> in such an amazingly calm and cool manner and with such excellent judgment that it inspired everyone who saw him and undoubtedly resulted in the saving of many lives. After

realizing that the ship could not be saved and that he was the senior surviving officer, he . . . directed abandoning ship and rescue of personnel until satisfied that all . . . that could be had been saved, after which he left his ship.

For his heroism Fuqua was awarded the Medal of Honor. Although 1,103 out of a crew of 1,400 were lost, he managed to save some of his men.

Only one battleship was able to get under way. The crew of *Nevada*, the oldest battleship at Pearl, were raising the American flag and playing "The Star-Spangled Banner" when Japanese planes attacked. The flag was ripped by gunfire, but the band completed the national anthem before the crew returned fire and began trying to escape the harbor. Hit by several bombs and a torpedo that tore a huge hole in her side, *Nevada* still managed to shoot down some attacking planes and get free of the mooring without the help of tugboats. "Down the ship channel she [went], fighting off dive bombers who concentrated on her, at one time surrounded by a curtain of smoke and spray so dense that spectators thought her gone; but most of the bombs were near misses. [*Nevada* was] a proud and gallant sight."

St. Louis reported shooting down two or three Japanese planes, and Captain Rood was finally able to back his ship out into the harbor ninety minutes after the first attack. Quickly picking up speed in the chaotic harbor, *St. Louis* rammed and broke a steel cable tying a dredge to the dock. Seeing that some destroyers and *St. Louis* were trying to reach the ocean, and fearing that *Nevada* might sink and block the channel, her officers ran her aground and she settled to the bottom. By now moving at twenty-eight miles per hour, *St. Louis* saw a submarine fire two torpedoes at her. Fortunately both hit a reef and exploded harmlessly. *St. Louis* returned fire and steamed out to sea, where Captain Rood gathered some destroyers into an attack group and went hunting the Japanese aircraft carriers that were reported to still be in the area. In fact, the carriers were hundreds of miles north of Pearl Harbor steaming toward Japan at top speed. *St. Louis* had left her four scout planes at Ford Island naval base when she raced to sea, but during the attack two of them managed to take off without their gunners. Although unarmed, the pilots tried to distract the Japanese bombers from the defenseless ships and port facilities. *St. Louis* and the destroyers searched for the Japanese carriers for three days before returning to the shattered Pacific Fleet. During the attack *St. Louis* had fired some sixteen thousand rounds of ammunition and possibly destroyed three enemy planes and a miniature submarine. Because she suffered no casualties and was only hit by a few Japanese bullets, her crew began calling her "Lucky Lou." To bring her up to wartime strength, about one hundred crewmen from the damaged *Nevada* were transferred to *St. Louis*. Captain Rood reported: "the whole ship performed to a degree of perfection that exceeded my most optimistic anticipation. [I have] the highest praise . . . for their conduct, devotion to duty, willingness and coolness under fire and during the following days of most exhausting operations. . . . This fine enthusiasm and spirit continues undiminished."

In just two hours the U.S. Navy had suffered three times as many casualties as during the entire Spanish-American and First World Wars.

When the *St. Louis* returned to Pearl Harbor, she was assigned to escort shiploads of wounded back to California. She then convoyed fresh troops back to Hawaii. Admiral Chester Nimitz, new commander of the Pacific Fleet, was already planning a counterattack against the Japanese. Admiral "Bull" Halsey volunteered to lead the attack, and *St. Louis* protected carrier *Yorktown* during air attacks on Japanese bases in the Marshall Islands in early February.

With so few warships available to fight the Japanese in

St. Louis escaping from Pearl Harbor under fire.
(National Archives and Records Administration)

the vast Pacific, *St. Louis* spent the first months of the war racing from task to task. In February 1942 she returned to Pearl Harbor to again escort convoys between Hawaii and California. She then returned to the New Hebrides Islands near New Guinea and Australia. By now Philippine president Manuel Quezon, having given General Douglas MacArthur a personal gift of a half million dollars to thank him for his attempt to defend the Philippines, had fled into exile. *St. Louis* escorted the passenger liner *President Coolidge* carrying President Quezon, which raced to San Francisco at top speed to outrun any Japanese submarines. *St. Louis* and *President Coolidge* arrived on May 8, 1942.

The very next day *St. Louis* steamed back toward Pearl Harbor to join a convoy taking marines and warplanes to reinforce the little American garrison on Midway Island. The convoy arrived on May 25. Brilliant American intelli-

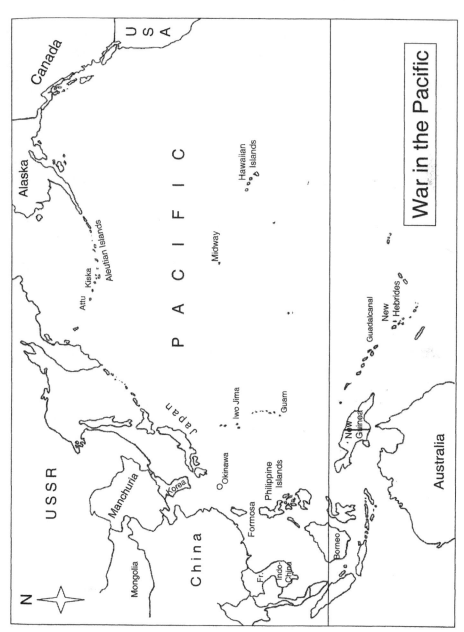

Pacific Theater, World War II. (Courtesy Lieutenant Colonel Steve Oluic)

gence had broken the Japanese naval codes, and the navy knew that the Japanese were planning to attack Midway. Just a few days after *St. Louis*'s departure, on June 4, American carriers surprised the Japanese and sank four of the six big Japanese carriers that had been involved in the attack on Pearl Harbor six months earlier. In an attempt to distract the United States, the Japanese had landed troops on Kiska and Attu in the Aleutian Islands. After dropping reinforcements on Midway in late May, *St. Louis* rushed to defend the Alaskan islands. For the next two months, while Japanese and Allied soldiers were locked in bloody battle in the mountain jungles of New Guinea, *St. Louis* patrolled the dangerous Alaskan waters, plagued by thick fog and terrible storms, searching in vain for Japanese supply ships. Only in early August did the weather clear enough for *St. Louis* to aim her big guns at Kiska, shell the Japanese troops with her main battery of six-inch guns, and cover the reoccupation of Adak Island by army troops.

By this time, far to the south in the Solomon Islands, American marines had landed on Guadalcanal, and American cruisers and destroyers were fighting bloody night duels with Japanese warships as the two navies struggled to supply their forces on the island. *St. Louis* remained in Alaska until the end of October 1942 and then returned to San Francisco for a quick overhaul. Captain Rood, who had commanded *St. Louis* since Pearl Harbor, left the ship for his next assignment while she was at San Francisco. In early December Captain Colin Campbell took *St. Louis* with a convoy of troop transports to New Caledonia in the Coral Sea between the Solomon Islands and Australia.

Japanese and American troops were still locked in battle on Guadalcanal, and the navies continued their deadly struggle in the surrounding waters. In early July 1943 *St. Louis* and the other cruisers and carriers of Task Force 18 bombarded Japanese troops on New Georgia Island near Guadalcanal to support American landings. On the pitch-black night of July 5–6, *St. Louis* and the other Allied ships caught Japanese destroyers rushing reinforcements to New Georgia. *St. Louis* was hit by an enemy torpedo that failed to explode, confirming her crew's opinion that she was "Lucky Lou." Captain Campbell later received the Navy Cross for his actions. A week later, Task Force 18 again met a Japanese force at the Battle of Kolombangara. In this battle, *St. Louis* was again hit by a torpedo, and this time she was not so lucky. It blew a large hole in her bow but caused no serious casualties. Captain Campbell's leadership in this action earned him the Silver Star, and *St. Louis* earned another trip to San Francisco for repairs.

While the ship was in California, Captain Campbell was replaced by Captain R. H. Roberts, who took *St. Louis* back to the Solomons in mid-November to support marine landings and bombard Japanese soldiers on Bougainville and the Green Islands. On the evening of February 14, 1944, *St. Louis* was attacked by six Japanese carrier bombers. After five near misses, she was hit in a crew compartment by a bomb that killed twenty-three sailors and wounded twenty. Both her airplanes were crippled, and the fire drove the crew from her rear engine room. After another air attack, *St. Louis* withdrew while her crew repaired the damage.

In June, during the landings on Saipan, Guam, and Tinian, *St. Louis* stayed close to shore using her main six-inch guns to shell Japanese defenders. On July 7, a propeller shaft weakened by her earlier battles and close calls broke free, but *St. Louis* remained on station for three more weeks before again returning to California for overhaul.

By the time *St. Louis* returned to the South Pacific in mid-November, General Douglas MacArthur's Sixth U.S. Army had returned to Leyte Island in the Philippines, and one of the greatest air and naval battles of World War II had been raging for a month. In the Battle of Leyte Gulf the Japanese lost hundreds of warplanes, almost all their remaining skilled pilots, all four of their carriers, and three battleships. The land battle for the Philippines continued, but the Japanese fleet and air force were so weakened that they had only one strategy left. That strategy came into action just as *St. Louis* arrived back in Leyte Gulf. With their skilled pilots dead, and facing increasingly heavy and effective naval antiaircraft gunfire, the Japanese turned to suicide air attacks by kamikaze pilots who tried to crash their bomb-laden aircraft into American ships.

In her first two weeks off Leyte *St. Louis* beat back thirty-three air attacks. On November 27, 1944, she was again attacked by swarms of Japanese planes. After fighting off the first wave of a dozen attackers, *St. Louis* was immediately threatened by another ten bombers. Although hit and afire, one bomber crashed into *St. Louis*'s hangar and exploded on impact.

Several gun crews were killed, and fires broke out, but *St. Louis* continued to fight and dodge at top speed. She avoided two more burning Japanese planes in the next few minutes, but a third crashed into the sea so close that *St. Louis* lost twenty feet of her armor belt and began flooding. For two hours, while gunners shot down another kamikaze and *St. Louis* fought off torpedo attacks, the crew struggled to control the flooding, fight the fires, and treat the wounded. In all, the ship lost fifteen dead, one missing, twenty-one seriously wounded, and another twenty-two lightly wounded. According to her Navy Unit Commendation: "Constantly harassed by hostile suicide attackers . . . she rendered invaluable fire support to our assault forces and, although severely damaged . . . during one of the most vicious multiple kamikaze attacks of the war, continued in action after decisively routing the enemy with heavy casualties."

Captain Ralph Roberts was awarded the Legion of Merit, with his executive officer, a marine captain, and a sailor earning Silver Stars. Four others earned Bronze Stars. One of the wounded who earned the Purple Heart

St. Louis hit by a kamikaze.
(National Archives and Records Administration)

St. Louis crewmen fighting fire started by a kamikaze.
(National Archives and Records Administration)

was a Gunner's Mate Brickner of Boonville, Missouri.

After a quick trip to California for repairs, *St. Louis* rejoined the American carriers attacking the Japanese home islands in late March 1945. By now, the United States had recaptured the Philippines and had won Iwo Jima, but at the cost of almost seven thousand dead and twenty thousand wounded. During this battle the marines earned twenty-seven Medals of Honor, including one for Sergeant Darrell Cole of Flat River, Missouri. Almost all twenty-one thousand Japanese defenders fought to the death. The American forces attacking Iwo Jima were supported by a huge American battle fleet, which included both the oldest U.S. battleship—*Arkansas*—and the newest—*Missouri*.

Missouri, BB-63, was the last American battleship ever completed. She and her sisters, *Iowa, New Jersey,* and *Wisconsin,* represented the evolution of over two hundred years of naval strategic thinking, but by the time they entered the battle against Japan in the last months of the Second World War, military technology had passed them by. Designed during the great naval race of the 1930s between democratic England and America and totalitarian Germany and Japan, they were created to be the fastest, best protected, and most heavily armed ships possible. They were narrow enough to pass through the Panama Canal and fast enough to outrun any other battleship, which was essential to their most important wartime duty—protecting fast American aircraft carriers from Japanese air attack. While twentieth-century battleship design had always concentrated on the size and power of main guns, the *Iowa*s were covered with twenty five-inch guns and over a hundred smaller antiaircraft guns to defeat the swarms of Japanese fighters and bombers intent on sinking U.S. carriers.

Work on *Iowa* began at the Brooklyn Navy Yard in June 1940, and on January 6, 1941, the yard began building *Missouri*. After an unusually long construction time of three years, while higher priority carriers, submarines, destroyers, and light cruisers were hastily built, *Missouri* was finally launched on January 29, 1944. Ignoring Missouri's republican governor Forrest C. Donnel, President Roosevelt chose to honor the powerful democratic chairman of the congressional war production board investigating committee by asking Harry Truman's daughter, Margaret, to christen the newest battleship. Before an audience of over 20,000, including a live television audience at the General Electric propulsion plant in Schenectady, New York, which had built her huge 212,000-horsepower turbines, Senator Truman predicted: "The time will surely come when the people of Missouri will thrill with pride as the *Missouri* and her sister ships . . . sail into Tokyo Bay." By radio, Admiral Halsey added: "We have a date to keep in Tokyo. Ships like *Missouri* will provide the wallop to flatten Tojo and his crew." Margaret Truman then christened *Missouri* with a bottle of champagne made from Missouri grapes.

Although final construction took another six months, Senator Truman was bombarded by letters from Missourians asking for assignment to the ship. Most of the wartime crew of 2,700 officers and men were from new draftees from the East, with only a handful from the "Show-Me" state, but Harry's nephew John C. Truman, a thirty-one-year-old schoolteacher from Independence with three children, happened to be randomly assigned to *Missouri.*

Missouri was finally commissioned on June 11, 1944, five days after the Allied invasion of Normandy, and two months after *Wisconsin*, BB-64, joined the fleet. *Missouri* was the last of fifty-seven battleships in the U.S. Navy. Her first captain, William M. Callaghan, had participated in a training cruise aboard the Great White Fleet *Missouri* while a young Annapolis midshipman.

After a few months of training for her green crew and testing of her guns, engines, and other systems, *Missouri*

Missourians in original BB-63 *Missouri* crew.
(Harry S. Truman Library)

squeezed through the Panama Canal on November 18, 1944, and reached the American naval base at Ulithi in the Caroline Islands east of Leyte, Philippines, in mid-January. There she joined Vice Admiral Marc Mitscher's aircraft carriers as on February 16, 1945, they launched the first carrier air attacks on Japan since Jimmy Doolittle's 1942 Tokyo raid. On the same day a huge American fleet began bombarding Iwo Jima. *Missouri* and her carriers remained well offshore, with the battleship using her radar-controlled five-inch guns to beat off attacking Japanese airplanes. Steaming steadily and constantly alert, *Missouri* traveled over eight thousand miles in February alone. *Missouri* and *St. Louis* screened the American carriers attacking the Japanese home islands and acted as "armored oilers," repeatedly refueling their thirsty short-range destroyer escorts. Joined by her sisters *New Jersey* and

Gun drill on *Missouri:* note shells in upper right.
(National Archives and Records Administration)

Wisconsin, Missouri shelled Okinawa in late March with her sixteen-inch main batteries from twenty thousand yards offshore. In early April, a kamikaze aircraft carrying a five hundred-pound bomb penetrated *Missouri*'s wall of defensive fire. One of sixteen aircraft launched from a base in southern Japan, the plane hit the side of the battleship just below the open gunmounts on the main deck, exploding with a huge and spectacular cloud of black smoke.

Fortunately the bomb fell into the ocean without detonating. A wing and the body of the pilot, probably nineteen-year-old Setsuo Ishino, landed on the deck. In the heat of the battle the crew began to throw the body overboard,

A kamikaze hitting *Missouri*. (Naval Historical Center)

Closeup of a kamikaze exploding on *Missouri*.
(National Archives and Records Administration)

Missouri Captain
William M. Callaghan.
(Naval Historical Center)

but Captain Callaghan, who had lost a brother to the Japanese, ordered his crew to give the pilot a proper burial at sea. Captain Callaghan never mentioned the episode again, but fifty-six years later American veterans identified the Japanese pilots involved and invited the survivors to a ceremony aboard *Missouri* at Pearl Harbor on April 12, 2001, to honor Callaghan's chivalry. Two days after the kamikaze hit *Missouri*, President Franklin Roosevelt died and his new vice president, Harry Truman, became the thirty-third president.

Heavy attacks continued around the clock, and during the Okinawa campaign the navy suffered 4,900 killed and 4,800 wounded. Both *Missouri* and *St. Louis* dodged close calls while all around them some 200 ships were hit, and, of those, 34 sank. The crews worked under terrible strain for weeks on end, with men and equipment suffering from the constant danger and action as the Japanese carried out 1,900 suicide attacks. *Missouri* shot down 5 enemy planes and helped to destroy 6 others, and *St. Louis* destroyed 4 and helped shoot down another 4. Captain John Griggs of *St. Louis* won the Silver Star for commanding the cruiser during the Okinawa battle.

In early June, the fleet was hit by an eighty-mile-an-hour typhoon with one hundred-foot waves, which tore one hundred feet off the bow of the new heavy cruiser *Pittsburgh.* According to a *Missouri* sailor, the battleship, even though three times heavier than *Pittsburgh:* "wallowed around . . . like a ping-pong ball in a bathtub with a baby playing with it" but suffered no serious damage.

In mid-July, *Missouri, Iowa,* and *Wisconsin* shelled steel mills in Hokkaido from over fifteen miles offshore, and hit other targets on following days with 2,700 pound shells from their main guns. The bombardment was so terrifying that most civilians fled and many workers refused to return to their posts. By now, American ships and planes could operate freely around the Japanese islands, but the military government still refused to surrender. To end the war Truman ordered the use of a new weapon, and on August 6, 1945, an army B-29 bomber dropped an atomic bomb on Hiroshima. Three days later a second bomb hit Nagasaki, and the Japanese emperor told his supreme war council to accept Allied surrender terms.

On August 15, the emperor broadcast a surrender order to the Japanese people and military, and President Truman announced the end of the war. In celebration, Admiral Halsey ordered the crew to blow *Missouri's* steam whistle, which jammed open until engineers could disconnect the steam line. The next day British Pacific Fleet commander Sir Bruce Fraser came aboard and awarded Halsey a knighthood of the British Empire. Two hundred *Missouri* sailors were given shore duty as part of the initial American military force occupying the Japanese islands. American newspapers began reporting that the formal Japanese surrender would take place on *Missouri* in Tokyo Bay, but even *Missouri*'s new captain, Stuart "Sunshine" Murray, only learned of the honor when his wife complained in a letter, "why don't you tell me about these things instead of letting me read it in the newspapers?"

Beneath their joy and relief at the end of the war, the Allies were concerned that diehard Japanese might launch further suicide attacks. Halsey ordered his forces to shoot down any Japanese intruders "in a friendly sort of way." Japanese harbor pilots came aboard *Missouri* under tight guard to show her officers the safe way into Tokyo Bay, and the Americans insisted a Japanese destroyer lead Allied battleships *Missouri, Iowa,* and *Duke of York* into the bay on August 29 as the crew stood by their guns on full alert against possible Japanese treachery. In preparation for the historic ceremony, the U.S. Naval Academy sent the flag flown by Commodore Matthew Perry's flagship, *Mississippi,* during her visit to Tokyo in 1853. Too fragile to be flown, the flag was displayed while by some accounts *Missouri* flew the flag that had flown over the U.S. Capitol on December 7, 1941.

On the morning of September 2, 1945, General of the Army Douglas MacArthur and Fleet Admiral Chester Nimitz came aboard *Missouri* to receive the Japanese surrender. The ship was crowded with crewmen, Allies, including former prisoners of war, and hundreds of journalists and photographers. One of the defeated Japanese remembered: "A million eyes seemed to beat on us with the million shafts of a storm of arrows barbed with fire. I felt them sink into my body with a sharp physical pain. Never have I realized that staring eyes could hurt so much."

At the end of the brief surrender ceremony, which was broadcast live around the world, General MacArthur concluded: "Let us pray that peace be now restored to the world and that God will preserve it always. Your sons and

Japanese boarding *Missouri* to sign World War II surrender. (National Archives and Records
Administration)

daughters have served you well and faithfully . . . they are
homeward bound."

The ceremony was followed by a flyover by a massive
fleet of hundreds of navy carrier planes and army B-29
bombers.

As MacArthur had promised, for most of the navy the
first order of business was getting the troops home. The
crew celebrated the surrender with a turkey dinner, welcome after months of monotonous and skimpy battle
rations, then *Missouri* left Tokyo Bay on September 6 and
picked up fifteen hundred marines on Guam for the happy
journey home. The already crowded wartime crew was

even more cramped with the additional passengers, and the officers tried to keep the men entertained with movies, boxing matches, and other contests as they rode the "Magic Carpet" home. The war was not over for everybody, however, and the weary veteran *St. Louis* stayed on station off the China coast as flagship of the Yangtze River Patrol Force. In October the cruiser finally joined Operation Magic Carpet, carrying eight hundred troops back to San Francisco on the first of three passenger runs that kept her disappointed crew on duty through the Christmas holidays. *St. Louis* had fought the Pacific war from the first minute to the last, earning eleven Battle Stars for her service. As her Navy Unit Citation said: "A resolute and sturdy veteran, complemented by skilled and aggressive officers and men, *St. Louis* rendered distinctive service, sustaining and enhancing the finest traditions of the United States Naval Service."

St. Louis finally reached Philadelphia in February 1946, and was decommissioned in June. In 1951 she was sold to the Brazilian navy, where she served as *Almirante Tamandare* until 1977. The Brazilians then donated the ship's wheel, battle flags, and builder's plaque to former crewmen and residents of St. Louis who wished to preserve her memory. After an unsuccessful American fund-raising effort to "save the 'Lucky Lou'" as a war memorial, the Brazilians sold her to a Hong Kong scrap dealer. On August 24, 1980, while being towed around the Cape of Good Hope, she capsized and sank.

CHAPTER FIVE

The Cold War

World War II ended as the Great War had ended twenty-seven years earlier, with relief, joy, demobilization of the great armies and navies, and the hope for a peaceful future. Harry Truman was proud of the battleship christened by his daughter and named for his state, and even more proud that after the Japanese surrender *Missouri* was the most famous battleship in the world. *Missouri* was thus the star attraction of a great naval review and victory celebration in New York at the end of October. To the president's disappointment, however, his nephew John and some 30 percent of the crew left the ship in Norfolk to return to civilian life. After workmen installed a plaque on the deck to mark the spot on which the surrender had taken place, the ship sailed up the East Coast to New York. On October 27, after a triumphal parade through the streets of the city, President Truman, his daughter, Margaret, and New York governor Thomas Dewey toured the ship. Sitting at the Tokyo Bay surrender table and signing *Missouri*'s guest book, Truman declared this the happiest day of his life. He then announced the bar open and drank a glass of bourbon with Captain Murray before reviewing the great fleet at anchor in the Hudson River.

During the ten-day celebration, some 750,000 New Yorkers toured the ship, leaving graffiti everywhere and stealing souvenirs. Someone even reached through a porthole and stole Captain Murray's uniform hat off his desk.

Harry S. Truman aboard the *Missouri* on what he called
"the happiest day of my life." (Harry S. Truman Library)

As a junior officer said, some visitors "just wanted to grub and grab." After coping with the horde of visitors, the crew got a rest as *Missouri* returned to her birthplace at the Brooklyn Navy Yard for an overhaul. Captain Murray was succeeded by St. Louis native Roscoe Hillenkoetter. The 1919 Annapolis graduate had served at sea in destroyers, cruisers, and battleships and as naval attaché at the American embassy in Paris. He had been in France when the Germans captured Paris in 1940, and in 1941 had been assigned as executive officer of battleship *West Virginia* at Pearl Harbor. *West Virginia*'s captain was killed in the attack on December 7, and Hillenkoetter was wounded, but he kept the ship from capsizing as she sank. African American cook Doris Miller won fame and the Navy Cross for courage during the attack. Aside from his diplomatic skill and courage under fire, Captain Hillenkoetter showed his character and integrity as a leader when the St. Joseph Lead Company of Flat River, Missouri, offered *Missouri* a silver sculpture of the state seal in January 1946. Hillenkoetter led a delegation of crewmen made up of Missourians to receive the gift from governor Phil M. Donnelly. While in St. Louis, a civic group honored the crew at a party at the elegant Chase Hotel. Learning that one crewman was black, the hotel refused him entrance, until Hillenkoetter, probably remembering "Dorie" Miller at Pearl Harbor, insisted: "he's a member of the crew of *Missouri*. If he doesn't come, we don't come."

In the spring of 1946 Hillenkoetter took on another ceremonial mission of great diplomatic importance. The United States emerged from the Second World War with the largest, most efficient, most powerful navy and air force in the world. The ally with the largest army, the Soviet Union, had conquered Eastern Europe and Berlin but was ruled by the paranoid and suspicious dictator Joseph Stalin and a ruthless and aggressive communist party. In China and Korea, communist armies were seizing territory vacated by the retreating Japanese, and in Eastern Europe small groups of communists were taking control of the countries overrun by Soviet armies. Anxious to put the burden of war behind them, few Americans recognized the growing Soviet threat. In his famous "Iron Curtain" speech in Fulton, Missouri, on March 5, 1946, Winston Churchill warned that democracy in Greece was threatened by a civil war between communists and nationalists. Greece was strategically important to the British because of its proximity to the Suez Canal through which England's oil supplies passed. The U.S. Navy had already decided to show American military strength in the area by dispatching the battleship *Missouri* on a diplomatic mission to Istanbul. Hearing that *Missouri* would be passing Gibraltar on her way to Turkey, the American consul there wrote a letter reminding the navy of the first *Missouri*'s fate. The Turks were delighted at the visit by the famous battleship, even refurbishing Istanbul's red-light district to welcome the American sailors. The Turks also gave a lavish party for the officers during which belly dancers performed to the "Missouri Waltz." As an officer recalled: "All of us were just sitting there dying because we couldn't break out laughing."

The presence of *Missouri* encouraged the Turks to resist Soviet demands. The ship then visited Piraeus, Greece, reminding the communist rebels that American naval power could reach even around the Iron Curtain. In demonstrating the long reach of American power, *Missouri* was following the first modern battleship *Missouri*, which had entertained the Greek royal family during the visit of the Great White Fleet in 1909. Thanks in large measure to President Truman's strong support for Greek independence, the communists were defeated, and Greece remained the only nation in Eastern Europe free of Russian control.

Missouri impressed the Greeks and Turks (and Russians) as a powerful symbol of American military strength, but in

"Coach—Truman Athletic Club"
returning from Rio aboard *Missouri*.
(Harry S. Truman Library)

spite of the growing tension between the West and the
Soviet Union, the U.S. Navy was shrinking rapidly. Two
thousand ships were put into reserve, and seven thousand
scrapped or given to allies such as Brazil. Navy personnel
strength dropped from 3,400,000 in 1945 to 380,000 in 1950.
By then, the navy had only eleven carriers and one battleship—*Missouri*—and even *Missouri's* crew was only one-
third her wartime strength. With only 800 men, her captain
had barely enough crew members to keep her running.

Still, *Missouri* was President Truman's favorite, and in the summer of 1947 sailed to Rio de Janeiro, Brazil, as the U.S. and Latin American countries signed a mutual defense treaty. President Truman flew to Rio to sign the treaty, but on September 7, he boarded *Missouri* with wife, Bess, and daughter, Margaret, for the cruise back to Norfolk. Truman had a wonderful time, leading exercise classes in his "Coach—Truman Athletic Club" T-shirt, chatting with sailors about baseball during his morning walks around the deck, waiting in line in the dining halls, and even joining the "victims" when the battleship crossed the equator.

New sailors had undergone the same initiation on the Great White Fleet *Missouri* forty years earlier, and King Neptune now accused Truman of the terrible offense of using a "despicable and unnatural means of travel" by flying to Rio for the conference. Truman was required to bribe the court with cigars, and Margaret had to sing "Anchors Aweigh" with six new ensigns. During the cruise Margaret ate with the crew, and teased captain Robert Dennison, maintaining that *Missouri* was her ship rather than his because she had christened it, and that she knew more about the crew than he did because she ate with them. Whether or not the crew enjoyed dining with Margaret, they did enjoy watching her sunbathe on deck.

If the cruise was a mini-vacation for Truman, he still kept a close eye on communist threats. While playing poker, he received a secret State Department message that Yugoslav communist General Josef Tito was threatening to invade the Italian town of Trieste. Truman ordered Captain Dennison to send a reply that "the SOB was going to have to shoot his way in."

The president and his family left *Missouri* at Norfolk, and one crewman remembered: "He was a very down-to-earth person. . . . He didn't stand on ceremony . . . he would sit there and talk to you about things that really mattered. . . . He worried about the little guy, the problems he was having. You really felt like he cared when he talked to you."

During the next two years the Cold War became more bitter. *Missouri* remained on the East Coast, and each summer took academy midshipmen on training cruises to Europe and the Caribbean. During a visit to England in 1949, three enterprising midshipmen talked their way into Winston Churchill's country house to pay him a visit. Churchill, a naval expert, spent several hours walking with them in his gardens talking about battleships. He then offered them drinks, cigars, and autographed copies of his books. Churchill's astonished security guard told the delighted midshipmen: "I have seen some of the great people come and just get ushered out the door. He treated you like I've never seen anyone treated. The only reason I can think for his hospitality is that he likes Americans, he likes young people, and he likes the navy."

In September 1949 Captain William Brown, who had commanded a destroyer in World War II, took command of *Missouri*. Brown did not welcome advice from his officers, many of whom were young and inexperienced. The ship left Norfolk on January 17, 1950, and through a combination of faulty navigation, equipment failure, and Brown's refusal to heed the warnings of his increasingly frantic senior crewmen and officers, *Missouri* ran almost half a mile up onto a shallow sandbar in full view of the admiral in his headquarters. The navy was terribly embarrassed that the president's favorite ship had gotten stuck in one of their largest and oldest ports. The Russians and even other American military services ridiculed the navy, and newspapers and radio spread the story around the world.

The navy was determined to prove its professionalism by quickly freeing *Missouri*. Sailors labored to unload ammunition, fuel, and stores to lighten her. Divers used high-pressure hoses to blast the sandbar from around her, and a

Missouri being pulled off Thimble Shoals.
(National Archives and Records Administration)

fleet of tugboats finally dragged her free on February 1. The ship's band played the "Missouri Waltz" and "Nobody Knows the Trouble I've Seen" while the crew raised huge battle flags and signaled "Reporting for Duty." Remarkably, the $100 million *Missouri* only suffered $50,000 damage, and repairs were completed in a week in drydock. After initially trying to blame his officers, Captain Brown took full responsibility at his court-martial and was convicted and disgraced. He later tried to commit suicide.

Congress tried to put *Missouri* in mothballs with her three *Iowa*-class sisters to pay for another aircraft carrier, but on June 25, 1950, the battleship was again called to war when 100,000 Russian-trained North Korean troops suddenly attacked South Korea. *Missouri* received urgent orders to take on hundreds of new crewmen and depart immediately for the Far East to support General MacArthur's struggling United Nations forces.

Racing south at twenty-eight miles per hour, *Missouri* ran through a hurricane off North Carolina that swept away her helicopters, smashed her boats, and had her rolling in the high winds and seas. She dodged another storm off Hawaii and ran through a typhoon near Japan before finally reaching South Korea on September 15, 1950, one month after leaving the East Coast. *Missouri* immediately began bombarding North Korean targets with her huge sixteen-inch shells, and soon United Nations commanders noticed that whenever *Missouri* appeared, enemy troops moved away from the coast to avoid her terrible guns. While enemy troops could hear the approach of attacking aircraft, *Missouri*'s first massive shells always hit with absolutely no warning, leaving huge explosions, great craters, and shocked and deafened survivors.

Reporters and film crews recorded her actions, and in late October famous comedian Bob Hope visited the ship to entertain her crew. *Missouri* raced up and down the Korean coastline, screening American carriers and attack-

Recruiting poster of *Missouri.*
(National Archives and Records Administration)

ing enemy targets. In late October she shelled North Korean factories at Chongjin near China and Russia. In late November, however, the Chinese joined the war, and United Nations forces were again pushed back. In December *Missouri* covered the safe evacuation of the American Third Infantry Division and many thousands of South Koreans from Hungnam. Through the bitter Korean winter *Missouri* could strike in weather that kept aircraft grounded or on their carriers, and she was particularly effective at accurately hitting railroads, bridges, tunnels, and enemy supply and troop concentrations. Allied soldiers praised the great range, accuracy, and power of her guns, noting "the destruction and damage caused by 16-inch gunfire was particularly gratifying."

At the end of March 1951 *Missouri* left Korea having fired almost three thousand sixteen-inch shells. As the first major warship to return from Korea, *Missouri*'s arrival in Long Beach, California, was broadcast on television. *Missouri* served again in Korea in the winter of 1952-1953 as the war was coming to an end, but tragedy struck when her captain, Warner R. Edsall, died of a heart attack on his bridge while bringing her into harbor in Japan in March 1953.

Dwight Eisenhower succeeded Harry Truman as president in January 1953, Joseph Stalin died in March, and the Korean War ended in July. *Missouri* and her sisters went back to routine training, including summer midshipman cruises, but it was now clear that they had been replaced by more advanced, powerful, and costly strategic weapons. President Eisenhower was forced to confront difficult budget choices, and battleships were an old-fashioned luxury when the United States had to build whole new types of weapons to face the Soviet threat. After thorough repair, preservation, and maintenance, *Missouri* was taken out of service and put into the Pacific Reserve Fleet in Puget Sound in February 1955. By 1958 her sisters *Iowa, New Jersey,* and *Wisconsin* had joined her, and for the first time in the twentieth century, the United States had no battleships on active duty. Even in reserve, however, *Missouri* continued to receive some 100,000 visitors each year who wanted to see the famous ship.

World War II had been a time of remarkable advances in military technology. The American navy perfected the use of fast task forces built around large aircraft carriers armed with scores of deadly bombers, torpedo planes, and fighters. The aircraft carrier became the new naval superweapon, and even the most modern battleships like *Missouri* were relegated to secondary roles using their radars and antiaircraft guns to defend the carriers from enemy air attack and their main batteries to support soldiers and marines fighting on shore. The carriers were now the most important, and the most expensive, warships, but the navy was faced with the huge expense of replacing now-obsolete wartime carriers with radically new ships specifically designed for modern jet aircraft. With their jet airplanes, small protective escort warships, and resupply ships, these supercarrier battle groups were able to project American power anywhere in the world, but at great cost.

The Soviets and United States were also developing the most terrifying weapon of the Cold War: nuclear tipped ballistic missiles. Once launched, these successors to the German V-2 could not be stopped by any defense and could reach their targets thousands of miles away within minutes. At first these ballistic missiles required large fixed launching bases and were vulnerable to counterattack by bombers or even enemy rockets, but in the mid-1950s the U.S. Navy began developing a ballistic missile that could be fired from a submerged submarine. By this time, the navy had harnessed nuclear power to drive ships. Once the U.S. Navy launched *Nautilus* in 1954 nuclear-powered submarines became, like aircraft carriers, jet airplanes, and ballistic missiles, major Cold War strategic weapons.

Missile-carrying submarines were especially attractive to American military leaders because of their invisibility. Even if a massive Soviet surprise attack crippled American strategic bombers and land-based ballistic missiles, the hidden submarines could retaliate and destroy the Soviet Union. These new superwarships were to be named for "distinguished Americans . . . known for their devotion to freedom," and the first ballistic missile submarine, SSBN-598, was named *George Washington*. Early missiles were dishearteningly unreliable, and while *George Washington* first successfully fired a Polaris missile while underwater on July 20, 1960, the next four missiles failed. To the dismay of her crew, the rockets fell back and crashed against *George Washington's* submerged hull.

Just a week before his assassination, on November 16, 1963, President John Kennedy watched a Polaris missile launch and wrote: "The Polaris firing I witnessed was a most satisfying and fascinating experience. It is still incredible to me that a missile can be successfully and accurately fired from beneath the sea. . . . The [effectiveness] of this weapon . . . as a deterrent is not debatable."

This first generation was quickly succeeded by new fleet ballistic missile submarines, nicknamed "boomers," designed from the start as strategic missile boats. *Lafayette*, SBN-616, the first of a class of thirty-one, was commissioned in 1963. Four hundred and twenty-five feet long and 33 feet in diameter, these boats weighed 7,250 tons, carried 16 Polaris missiles and a crew of 140 officers and men, and could "steam" at 34 miles per hour underwater and operate 900 feet below the surface. Their Westinghouse nuclear reactors generated some 15,000 horsepower, and each boat cost about $110 million. By this time, new Polaris A-3 missiles had a range of 2,500 miles with a payload of three 200-kiloton warheads. By comparison, the bombs that had destroyed Hiroshima and Nagasaki only had the power of 10 kilotons (10,000 tons) of dynamite.

The twelfth *Lafayette* boat, SSBN-629, *Daniel Boone,* was built at Mare Island Naval Shipyard in San Francisco Bay and was commissioned on April 23, 1964. During the next decades of the Cold War, *Daniel Boone* and her sister boomers continued their silent secret patrols, and because of their invisibility and invulnerability helped maintain the "balance of terror" that kept the superpowers at peace. *Daniel Boone* was the first boat armed with the new long-range, multiple-warhead Polaris A-3. The *Lafayette*s were designed for stealth and long life, and most outlasted the Cold War and the Soviet Union itself.

These submarines could go 400,000 miles between refuelings and were limited only by their crews' endurance. The boats could even generate their own oxygen from seawater. Indeed, in 1959, *Triton* had circled the world underwater, traveling 36,014 miles in 84 days. *Daniel Boone* and her sisters were thus given two identical crews. While the "blue" crew was on shore training and resting, the "gold" crew was on their seventy-day underwater patrol. Normally, the boomers would submerge as soon as they left their bases at Guam, Rota, Spain, and Holy Loch, Scotland, and go quietly to patrol areas within range of their targets in the Soviet Union. They would then await the command to launch their forty-eight nuclear warheads against Soviet cities, factories, or military bases, all the while remaining silent to avoid detection by Soviet attack submarines. By 1972, American ballistic missile submarines had completed some one thousand such patrols.

Having served faithfully and silently during the most dangerous years of the Cold War, all the *Lafayette*s were decommissioned and scrapped as Russia and the United States began to relax their suspicion of each other. *Daniel Boone* was decommissioned in February 1994, following the dissolution of the Soviet Union on December 25, 1991. Her nuclear fuel removed and her radioactive reactor buried at Hanford, Washington, she and her sisters were cut to pieces in accordance with Russian-American agreements.

Because of their stealth and the great power of their nuclear missiles, ballistic missile submarines changed the way that navies looked at undersea warfare. The Russians had assembled a huge fleet of attack submarines to counter the mighty American surface fleet of aircraft carriers and to threaten Atlantic supply lines essential to supporting American and allied armies defending Western Europe. In 1948, just after the Soviets tried to starve the Western allies out of Berlin, the Soviet navy had 250 submarines. In 1960, as *George Washington* was beginning her first patrol, the Russian submarine fleet numbered 437 boats, and the Soviets, too, were beginning to build ballistic missile submarines to threaten American cities. Although the U.S. Navy remained the most powerful in the world, it needed nuclear attack submarines to defend carriers, guard American boomers, shadow the Soviet surface navy, collect intelligence, and neutralize the growing Soviet fleet of ballistic missile boats.

The first of sixty-two fast, powerful, quiet attack boats, SSN-688, *Los Angeles*, entered the fleet on November 13, 1976. These boats are 362 feet long and 33 feet in diameter, weigh some 6,000 tons, can reportedly dive as deep as 1,500 feet, and have 35,000-horsepower reactors that drive them faster than 30 miles an hour submerged. They carry crews of around 130 officers and men and are armed with torpedoes and Tomahawk cruise missiles that can be fired from their regular torpedo tubes. The Tomahawk, with a range of up to 1,400 miles at a speed of 550 miles per hour, can be used to attack either ships or land targets with nuclear or high explosive warheads.

During the remainder of the Cold War as many as six sister ships a year were completed at Newport News Shipyard or the Electric Boat Division of General Dynamics Corporation at Groton, Connecticut. While General Dynamics

Jefferson City running on surface.
(Defense Visual Information Center)

charged only $221 million each for the first boats, prices rapidly rose to $496 million per boat by 1981 and reached $900 million by the end of the Cold War.

The forty-eighth *Los Angeles, Jefferson City,* SSN-759, was begun on September 21, 1987, at Newport News. She was launched on August 17, 1990, just weeks after Iraqi dictator Saddam Hussein invaded Kuwait and less than two months before a free Germany was reunited within NATO. She was finally commissioned on February 29, 1992, just two months after the collapse of the Soviet Union and the creation of the Russian republic. Her homeport is San Diego, California, and she is still patrolling with the Pacific Fleet. Since her commissioning, the American submarine fleet has been cut to fewer than twenty boomers and sixty attack submarines, but *Jefferson City* and her sisters remain alert.

The operations of American attack submarines are kept secret, but a number of stories have emerged about their dangerous Cold War missions and the silent undersea "war" between American and Soviet or Russian submariners. Because their mission is to "hide with pride" until ordered to launch their ballistic missiles against enemy targets, locating and shadowing boomers was the most critical mission for both American and Russian attack submarines. Sometimes, miscalculation or aggressive pursuit led to accidents. In December 1967 *Daniel Boone'* s sister *George C. Marshall,* SSBN-654, was hit by a submerged Soviet submarine in the Mediterranean, and in November 1974 another sister, *James Madison,* SSBN-627, hit a Soviet attack submarine while leaving the American ballistic submarine base at Holy Loch, Scotland. As late as February 1992, *Jefferson City*'s sister *Baton Rouge,* SSN-689, collided with a Russian submarine near the big Russian naval base at Murmansk in the Arctic above Norway.

Russian ballistic missile submarine patrol areas are in icebound northern "bastions" close to Russia. To operate in these frozen seas, later *Los Angeles* submarines like *Jefferson City* were built with reinforced sails for under-ice operations. To strengthen their offensive power, they were also equipped with twelve vertical launch tubes for Tomahawk cruise missiles, but these missiles were not fired against an enemy until after the Cold War had ended.

American submarines did not just stalk their Soviet targets; daring crews used their boats as "underwater U-2s" to collect intelligence on Soviet tactics, the performance of Soviet submarines and surface ships, and even on Soviet military plans. Specially equipped American submarines were able to tap into Russian undersea telephone cables and conduct other secret intelligence missions using spe-

PBR (Patrol Boat River), Vietnam. (Naval Historical Center)

cially trained crew members, divers, and even navy SEALs. The navy has also designed small submarines that ride in drydock shelters mounted piggyback on nuclear attack submarines until they reach their target areas.

While war never broke out between the Americans and Soviets during the Cold War, the forty-five years between the end of World War II and the collapse of the Soviet Union was by no means a time of peace for the U.S. Navy. Many sailors died while collecting intelligence on the Soviet Union and her allies, and many more died in the hot wars of the late twentieth century. The longest and most bloody of these wars was fought in Southeast Asia. By 1964, U.S. Navy ships were patrolling the Vietnamese coast looking for northern weapons supply boats, and soon

Harold Dale Meyerkord.
(Courtesy Dr. Marion P.
Meyer)

navy pilots were attacking North Vietnam from offshore
aircraft carriers. Most of the fighting was in South Vietnam.
The navy played a role there as well, manning a "brown
water navy" of small patrol boats in the Mekong River
delta. These little boats, with their small crews, operated in
much the same conditions that faced David Dixon Porter's
Eads gunboats during the Vicksburg campaign of 1862–
1863. Like *Cairo* and *St. Louis* on the Yazoo River, they were
terribly vulnerable to ambush as they crept up muddy,
narrow canals bordered by deep vegetation that could easily hide enemy soldiers. The sailors never knew whether
local villagers were harboring guerrilla fighters, and like
Porter's sailors, they fought in terrible heat and humidity
amid swarms of mosquitoes. As a sailor remembered:

"You really feel like a sitting duck when you're riding those boats . . . down the small canals. . . . The only trouble is [the Viet Cong] always gets the first punch."

Still, despite some two thousand enemy ambushes and many casualties, many young sailors loved the freedom and excitement of the little riverboats. One crew of a thirty-foot fiberglass, jet-propelled Patrol Boat River (PBR) taunted a passing "tin can" destroyer by singing:

> PBRs get all the pay,
> Get the tin can out of the way.
> PBRs roll through the muck,
> While tin can sailors suck!

One of the earliest U.S. Navy river advisors was Lieutenant Harold Dale Meyerkord from St. Louis, Missouri, a graduate of the University of Missouri. Fighting beside his Vietnamese allies in more than thirty firefights, he was wounded twice. Famed war correspondent Dickey Chapelle profiled him in a *National Geographic* magazine article on the "Water War in Vietnam." After Meyerkord died, on March 16, 1965, in a Viet Cong ambush while leading his boats, Chapelle described him as "audacious, ebullient . . . husband, father, leader and teacher of men . . . dead . . . on a muddy canal 9,000 miles from Missouri." On November 9, 1965, Secretary of the Navy Paul Nitze personally gave the navy's highest award for heroism, the Navy Cross, to his widow, Jane Schmidt Meyerkord, and his parents, Mr. and Mrs. Harold E. Meyerkord. Chapelle herself had been killed in Vietnam just five days earlier.

The navy moved quickly to honor Meyerkord. Less than a year later the keel was laid at San Pedro, California, for a new *Knox*-class frigate, DE-1058, *Meyerkord*. Launched on July 15, 1967, as the fifth in a class of forty-six antisubmarine ships, she was commissioned on November 28, 1969, and cost about $18 million. She was 438 feet long, weighed

3,000 tons, carried a crew of 220 officers and men, and was designed to fight Soviet submarines. Unfortunately, she and her sisters had a top speed of only 33 miles an hour and were thus slower than either American aircraft carriers or the newest Soviet November nuclear submarines. Still, she was the first ship named for a serviceman killed in Vietnam to return to fight in the same war. Beginning in March 1971 she served three times in Vietnamese waters, providing naval gunfire support with her single 5-inch gun. She also escorted American carriers in the western Pacific, protecting them from North Vietnamese airplanes or gunboats. *Meyerkord* also served as lifeguard if carrier planes crashed on landing or takeoff or sailors fell overboard.

Her last Vietnam tour began in January 1975 as the Republic of Vietnam was collapsing. After rescuing thirty-one crew members from a sinking freighter at the end of January, she joined "Operation Eagle Pull" evacuating Westerners from Phnom Penh, Cambodia. In April, she helped rescue Americans and Vietnamese in "Operation Frequent Wind" as Saigon fell to the victorious North Vietnamese. A month later, she was part of the carrier group supporting American military efforts to rescue the American crew of the freighter *Mayaguez* captured by Cambodian communists.

No longer required to support a war in southeast Asia, *Meyerkord* remained on duty in the Pacific. Now, however, aside from her responsibility to escort carriers, *Meyerkord* also rescued fishing boats and pleasure yachts in the stormy Pacific. Her crew underwent nuclear weapons training and inspection so *Meyerkord* could be equipped with nuclear antisubmarine warheads. They took this responsibility so seriously that in February 1981 the ship earned an outstanding overall nuclear weapons certification. Through the remainder of the Cold War, *Meyerkord* continued to operate in the Pacific from her San Diego base, frequently cruising to the western Pacific and escorting American carrier groups. In 1983 she was one of the ships sent to recover wreckage from the Korean Airlines 747 jumbo jet KAL-007 shot down by Soviet fighters for straying into Soviet territory. *Meyerkord*'s crew won a Meritorious Unit Citation for this grim duty.

Even without the war in Vietnam, the United States faced many challenges in the 1970s and 1980s. The Soviets continued to encourage communists to seize power in countries in southeast Asia, the Middle East, Africa, and South and Central America. Wars between Israel and her Muslim neighbors inspired Islamic radicalism and terrorism, and in the 1970s Middle East oil producers began using oil prices as a weapon against the West. In Iran, radicals overthrew the pro-Western Shah, occupied the American embassy in Tehran, and took American diplomats hostage. At the end of 1979 the Soviets sent troops into Afghanistan and began their decade-long war against Muslim fighters. Finally, in September 1980, Iraqi dictator Saddam Hussein attacked Iran, beginning a war that went on for a decade and threatened Western oil shipments through the Persian Gulf. The United States was thus faced with growing Muslim radicalism and Middle East unrest while the Soviet Union appeared to be an increasingly aggressive military and ideological global threat.

The war in Vietnam and inflation had strained the navy's budget, and there had been repeated efforts to scrap the four mothballed *Iowa* sisters. President Ronald Reagan felt that their awesome power and reputation would be valuable additions to the fleet. Despite strong objections to the cost of updating and manning these old warships, and concern about their vulnerability to new weapons like nuclear cruise missiles, he ordered them back into service.

In May 1984 *Missouri* was towed to Long Beach for her $468-million reactivation. To supplement her original 16-inch guns, she was equipped with 8 Tomahawk launchers as well as 4 Phalanx anticruise missile guns. She also received new radars, air-conditioning, and a modern "combat engagement center" from which her captain could command during combat. *Missouri's* modernization was particularly delicate because of the need to protect the historic World War II surrender plaque and a large mural in the admiral's quarters used by Harry Truman on his return from Rio in 1947. The admiral's quarters were converted into the new electronic combat control center, but the mural remained. Many 5-inch and other obsolete antiaircraft guns were removed to allow space for Tomahawk launchers, but the navy was still forced to salvage many old parts from museum battleships like *North Carolina* to return *Missouri's* machinery to operation.

The first of *Missouri's* new crew arrived in September 1985. Her new senior sailor, Master Chief John Davidson, had served aboard *Missouri* forty years earlier during her Istanbul and Rio cruises in 1946 and 1947. He was so anxious to rejoin the ship rather than retire that "I told them I'd pay them to let me serve." *Missouri* was recommissioned in San Francisco on May 10, 1986. Captain Lee Kaiss chose sailors from Missouri to stand the first watch, and Margaret Truman Daniel was again the ship's sponsor. At the commissioning, Captain Kaiss said: "On October 27, 1945, when President Harry S. Truman stepped aboard . . . he said 'this is the happiest day of my life.'. . . I know exactly how he felt." At a dinner and fireworks display for the crew sponsored by the state of Missouri, Margaret addressed them: "Captain Kaiss and the men of *Missouri* . . . please take good care of my baby." As a sailor remembered, "the crew went nuts" and gave her a standing ovation. The only sour note of the celebration was that Governor John Ashcroft had resisted returning the ship's silver service until, according to Captain Kaiss, the navy was prepared to send federal marshals to Jefferson City to reclaim it.

In September, *Missouri* set off on an around-the-world goodwill cruise. After laying a wreath at Pearl Harbor's

Arizona memorial, *Missouri* retraced the Great White Fleet's route and again saluted the famous leper colony on Molokai. *Missouri* then visited Sydney, Australia, where her crew received as warm a welcome as had greeted the Great White Fleet in 1908. Hundreds of thousands of people mobbed the ship, and the crewmen were treated so well that sailors from other ships began sewing *Missouri* patches on their uniforms to get free drinks from the hospitable Australians. A cousin of British admiral Lord Fraser, who had represented Great Britain at the Japanese surrender in 1945, spoke for the gratitude of many Australians for America's role in World War II when she visited the surrender plaque and said: "I feel I should get down on my knees and kiss the deck."

In early November *Missouri* passed through the Suez Canal and again visited Istanbul, where forty years earlier she had encouraged the Turkish and Greek governments to resist communist aggression. After crossing the Atlantic she squeezed through the Panama Canal one last time, losing some paint in the process. As her captain recalled: "It sounded—magnified by ten thousand times—like fingers going down a blackboard. It was awful, the loudest screeching you ever heard in your life."

Missouri returned to Long Beach on December 19, 1986. The cruise was the first around-the-world voyage by an American battleship since that made by the Great White Fleet, and it would be the last. *Missouri* had entertained huge crowds at every port, showing the American flag and reminding the world of America's great naval power.

During her cruise, *Missouri* had stayed clear of crisis points then occupying the attention of the U.S. military. In the Persian Gulf, the bitter war between Iran and Iraq was threatening Western tankers carrying oil to Europe and Japan, as both sides fired on ships leaving the other's ports.

In January 1987 Kuwait asked the United States to allow Kuwaiti tankers to fly the American flag so the U.S. Navy could protect them from Iranian mines, armed speedboats, and Chinese-made Silkworm cruise missiles. The U.S. Navy quickly increased its presence in the Persian Gulf. On May 17, the American frigate *Stark* was badly damaged by two French-built Exocet cruise missiles mistakenly fired by an Iraqi fighter plane. Although thirty-seven sailors were killed, the crew managed to save the ship. It was clear that modern cruise missiles were a deadly threat to both tankers and thin-skinned frigates and aircraft carriers. The navy thus ordered the heavily armored *Missouri* into the tanker war. As one of *Missouri*'s officers said: "we knew we were sending a very powerful signal by sending the battleship up there, and it wasn't lost on anybody."

In early October 1987, *Missouri* led a convoy of tankers and escort frigates through the narrow Strait of Hormuz into the Persian Gulf. As they passed Iranian Silkworm batteries, *Missouri*'s sensors warned that missile-targeting radars were tracking them. With her own main sixteen-inch guns aimed at the batteries, *Missouri*'s captain James Carney ordered her crew inside her armor while he remained on the bridge during the night-long transit. The Iranian guns remained quiet, and the ships passed safely. *Missouri* remained near the strait while the tankers sailed on to Kuwait escorted by smaller warships. As they neared Kuwait the next day, the tanker *Sea Isle City* was hit by a Silkworm.

Missouri escorted six more convoys through the dangerous strait past the Iranian missile sites, but her crew grew frustrated by the lack of action, the burning Arabian heat, and the lack of mail from home. Twice during *Missouri*'s hundred days on station, her captain allowed "steel-beach" parties on the helicopter landing pad at which each sailor was allowed two beers. The battleship finally left the war zone on November 24 and arrived at the island naval base of Diego Garcia in the Indian Ocean to discover that an officer had written the newspaper advice columnist

"Dear Abby" complaining that his sailors were receiving so little mail. In response to Abby's appeal, tens of thousands of people wrote, and *Missouri*'s men were buried in mail. *Missouri* reached Sydney, Australia, and received another hearty welcome. So many Australians offered hospitality that many sailors and marines spent Christmas Eve with one family and Christmas Day with another.

In April 1989 the men of the four American battleships were shocked by the explosion of one of *Iowa*'s sixteen-inch guns, which killed many in the turret. After careful investigation and testing of the navy's forty-year-old gunpowder, *Missouri* was again allowed to fire her main battery in September. Her captain, John Chernesky, personally fired the first shot from inside her turret. Thereafter, he insisted on frequent gun drill to rebuild turret crew confidence.

In July 1989, while Chernesky was ashore, the navy allowed the singer Cher to film the music video for "If I Could Turn Back Time" aboard *Missouri*. To the crew's delight she wore such a skimpy costume that columnist Jack Anderson complained: "if battleships could blush, *Missouri* would be bright red." Chernesky refused to blame his officers for the scandal, and whenever *Missouri* refueled at sea he played the song over the loudspeakers. A tough but popular officer, Chernesky was replaced in June 1990 by Captain Lee Kaiss, who had recommissioned *Missouri* in 1986. In July, with the Cold War ending, the navy again decided to deactivate *New Jersey* and *Iowa,* and it warned Kaiss that *Missouri* was next.

CHAPTER SIX

A New World, New Threats, and New Ships

The Iran-Iraq war had ended with Saddam Hussein's Iraq the strongest military power in the region, but saddled with a huge $37 billion war debt. Because of American concern about Iran's militant hostility, Presidents Reagan and Bush had supported Iraq, providing aid and intelligence to help fight Iran. The United States even forgave the deadly attack on *Stark* as a case of mistaken identity. Now, Saddam began demanding financial aid from other oil-rich Arab countries and belittling American power and determination.

On August 2, 1990, Iraqi Republican Guard divisions overwhelmed the small Kuwaiti military and within two days captured the whole country. *Missouri* was quickly ordered to the region. Her crew received chemical warfare training, and the ship was equipped with unmanned Pioneer drones equipped with TV cameras to serve as spotters for her gunfire. Because both Iran and Iraq had scattered thousands of mines throughout the Persian Gulf, mine disposal experts also joined the crew. With her sixteen hundred-man crew still being trained, *Missouri* left Long Beach on November 13. Because of her fame, and because the navy had already announced her retirement, CNN broadcast her departure live. On January 3, 1991, she passed through the Strait of Hormuz into the Persian Gulf. Six days later, *Missouri's* antimine team destroyed their first Iraqi mine. As a Vietnam veteran in her crew remembered: "That mine woke up the entire crew. Those of us who remembered, and [the young sailors] who didn't."

As the allied coalition assembled a great army to eject the Iraqis from Kuwait, the navy's experience during World War II and the Cold War proved very valuable. The navy had learned how to conduct a tight blockade during the Vietnam War when the fleet patrolled twelve hundred miles of Indochina coastline in Operation Market Time. Hundreds of Iraqi and other ships were inspected, with no casualties despite occasional Iraqi resistance. World War II and Vietnam had also taught the navy how to supply a combat fleet far from home.

Among the fleet of supply ships supporting coalition warships was the fleet oiler *Kansas City*, AOR-3, a member of the seven-ship *Wichita* class built by General Dynamics in Quincy, Massachusetts, during the Vietnam War. She had been commissioned in 1970 as a "multi-purpose replenishment ship" to carry fuel, ammunition, food, and other supplies to the fleet at sea. Able to carry over twenty thousand tons of supplies, and with a top speed of almost twenty-three miles per hour, she could keep pace with battleships and carriers. She also carried helicopters to supply warships from the air. *Kansas City* kept *Missouri* and other coalition warships "topped off" with ammunition and fuel and served until 1994 when she was finally decommissioned.

As the armies and navies assembled to drive the Iraqi invaders from Kuwait, General Norman Schwarzkopf and Chairman of the Joint Chiefs General Colin Powell planned a great deception to trick Saddam into concentrating his attention and armies on Kuwait itself. Iraqi forces were constructing a strong defensive "Saddam Line" of fortifications south of Kuwait City and fortifying the coastline with bunkers as the Germans had done in Normandy in

Gulf War propaganda flyer warning of marine assault.
(Naval Historical Center)

1944. Schwarzkopf put two marine divisions on the Saudi-Kuwait border and assembled marine amphibious forces supported by *Missouri* and *Wisconsin* offshore. The United States dropped thousands of propaganda leaflets on Iraqi positions showing a cartoon of a terrifying marine tidal wave backed by aircraft carriers as Iraqi soldiers fled for their lives.

In the early hours of January 17, 1991, President Bush ordered massive air attacks on Iraq. The navy launched waves of carrier aircraft and Tomahawk cruise missiles as part of the biggest air attack since World War II. *Missouri* fired 6 Tomahawks at Baghdad, and an Australian naval officer watching the nighttime attacks called them "altogether a most incredible and unforgettable sight." In the first day, the navy launched 122 Tomahawks. *Missouri*'s crew could listen to live CNN broadcasts from Baghdad as the Tomahawks hit their targets.

At the end of January, as air attacks continued, Iraqi troops from Kuwait captured the deserted Saudi border town of Khafji. The Saudis were deeply offended by this

Iraqi insult, and Saudi and Qatari tanks supported by marine helicopters soon recaptured the town. *Missouri*, guided by Saudi pilots, crept through water so shallow that she only had three feet of clearance under her keel to get within range of Iraqi positions. Using her drone to find targets, she fired almost two hundred rounds from her sixteen-inch guns. The crew was able to watch the shells hit with the drone's TV cameras, and the video was broadcast to every television set on the battleship. The Iraqis tried to hide their positions, but the drone watched an Iraqi truck drive from bunker to bunker delivering supplies. *Missouri*'s crew plotted the route, and then hit the concealed bunkers with sixteen-inch shells.

The shallow Kuwaiti coastal waters made it impossible for modern navy ships to get close enough to use their five-inch guns, and the fleet was fortunate that President Reagan had insisted on recalling the battleships to active duty. With their heavy armor they were relatively safe from mines and cruise missiles, and their sixteen-inch guns could deliver devastating long-range blows to coastal defenses. In early February, *Wisconsin* and *Missouri* moved close to the Kuwaiti border and shelled radars, artillery, and troop bunkers. Apparently angry that the navy was getting such good publicity with its Tomahawks and battleships, General Schwarzkopf ordered his navy commander Vice Admiral Stanley Arthur to "stop firing the goddam [sixteen-inch guns of the] battleships" or any more Tomahawks.

Still, the battleships had a vital role in Schwarzkopf's attack plans. Once the ground war began, the Iraqis had to believe that the marines would storm ashore to recapture Kuwait. As Arthur said: "I knew that the Iraqis always expected to see a battleship with amphibious landings. All I had to do was start moving the battleships and then line [our] fine marines . . . up behind them, and there was no doubt in anybody's mind that we were coming."

On the morning of February 23, 1991, *Wisconsin* began shelling Iraqi defenses as Arab troops and two marine divisions began advancing into Kuwait. Late that night, from a small coastal area that had been swept of mines, *Missouri* began shelling Iraqi troops on Faylaka Island outside Kuwait's harbor. Steaming back and forth inside the mineswept safe zone, *Missouri* sometimes had to aim her forward turrets back "over her shoulder" to keep Iraqi positions under fire.

The next day the main coalition ground assault began. As the heavy army divisions stormed through the Iraqi desert destroying Iraqi tanks and racing to surround and cut off Saddam's occupying army, the battleships and marine ground divisions continued to attack Iraqi forces in Kuwait. Marines cut their way through Saddam Line minefields and moved toward Kuwait's airport "like a snake getting ready to strike." In the early hours of February 25, *Missouri* began shelling Kuwait's Ash Shuaybah seaport. To paralyze the Iraqi reserves waiting for a marine amphibious assault, *Missouri* pretended to be both battleships. She first fired one sixteen-inch shell every forty-five seconds, but after two hours built up to a shell every five seconds as if the ships were softening up the beach so the marines could storm ashore.

During the bombardment, Iraqi batteries fired two Silkworms at *Missouri.* One crashed harmlessly into the sea, but the crew saw a huge fireball as the second raced toward the battleship at over six hundred miles per hour. Her bridge crew scrambled for cover, but British destroyer *Gloucester* shot down the Silkworm as it passed behind *Missouri.* The Silkworm explosion was so bright that *Missouri*'s lookouts at first thought that *Gloucester* herself had exploded. *Missouri*'s Phalanx antimissile guns had locked onto the Silkworm, but the Phalanx computer had decided that the passing missile was no threat and thus had not fired. During World War II hundreds of crewmen had manned dozens of antiaircraft guns throwing storms of lead at oncoming threats. Now, four computer-guided unmanned guns and her small escort ships were *Missouri's* only antiaircraft protection. Her drone quickly spotted the hidden Silkworm battery, which *Missouri* destroyed with thirty sixteen-inch shells. During a later false alarm, *Missouri* suffered her only Gulf War casualty when a sailor was slightly wounded by Phalanx fire from an escort frigate.

As the First Marine Division approached Kuwait's airport, *Wisconsin* shelled Iraqi tank concentrations on the airfield. Her drone recorded the destruction and showed Iraqi soldiers abandoning their vehicles to escape the gunfire. On February 27, marines liberated the empty American embassy. The next day, exactly one hundred hours after the ground war began, President George H. W. Bush ordered a ceasefire. On March 1, *Wisconsin* sent her drone over Faylaka Island where an Iraqi marine brigade was still dug in. Recognizing the drone, and knowing that sixteen-inch battleship shells would soon follow, Iraqi soldiers tried to surrender to the tiny unmanned, unarmed aircraft. U.S. Marines landed and captured fourteen hundred soldiers and over one hundred officers. Generals Powell and Schwarzkopf considered holding ceasefire talks on *Missouri* so that Saddam and the whole world would understand the extent of his defeat. They finally decided to meet Iraqi delegates in the middle of the desert to demonstrate that an international coalition rather than exclusively American power had won the war.

Missouri and *Wisconsin* left the Gulf in March, with *Wisconsin* immediately entering the reserve. Stopping at Pearl Harbor on her way home, *Missouri* welcomed sailors' family members for the final leg back to Long Beach. On May 9, in an impressive demonstration for the families, *Missouri* fired her huge sixteen-inch guns for the last time. The battleship returned to Long Beach to the warm welcome of waiting families. In the all-volunteer navy, more than half the crew were married, and during the six-month war deployment some fifty babies had been born. Captain Kaiss's wife, Veronica, arranged for the new mothers and their babies to be the first aboard to greet their returning husbands.

That summer and fall *Missouri,* again the only active battleship, made a final West Coast farewell cruise to Seattle, Vancouver, British Columbia, and San Francisco. Governor John Ashcroft and his son Andrew were aboard for the final leg from San Francisco back to Long Beach in October. While at Long Beach, *Missouri* was visited by actor Steven Seagal, then planning the movie *Under Siege* about terrorists capturing the battleship. Because the movie involved an officer betraying the ship to terrorists, neither the navy nor *Missouri's* officers were enthusiastic about helping the moviemakers. Action scenes were thus filmed on museum ship *Alabama* in Mobile Bay. Still, the film crew shot beautiful aerial film of *Missouri* leaving Long Beach in November on her way to Hawaii for the fiftieth anniversary of the Pearl Harbor attack, as well as film of the ceremonies at Pearl.

Everybody understood that the journey to Hawaii was *Missouri's* last cruise, and during the voyage a reporter from the *St. Louis Post-Dispatch* wrote an article on the ship and crew. As crewman John Lewis of Palmyra, Missouri, told him: "I'm losing a member of my family. Its really hard to accept and understand. . . . There are only two kinds of sailors in the navy. Those who have been on a battleship and those who wish they could."

On the morning of December 7, 1991, twelve hundred guests arrived, including President George Bush, who along with his wife, Barbara, briefly toured the ship. General Colin Powell and his wife also came aboard and were eagerly greeted by crew members, *Arizona* survivors, and other guests.

Upon her return to California, *Missouri* unloaded all her

Missouri returning to Pearl Harbor for the last time.
The *Arizona* Memorial is in the foreground.
(Defense Visual Information Center)

ammunition for the last time. Captain Kaiss had insisted that the battleship be fully armed on her Hawaii voyage. As the battleship entered Long Beach harbor for the last time, she was honored by whistle salutes from every ship in the port. *Missouri* was decommissioned for the last time on March 31, 1992, by Captain Lee Kaiss, who had presided at her recommissioning six years earlier. Among the guests at this sad ceremony was Missouri congressman Ike Skelton, whose father had served on the earlier *Missouri.* At the end of the ceremony her remaining six hundred crewmen filed off the ship, with Captain Kaiss being the last to depart. He was the last captain of the last American battleship.

Missouri was towed to the reserve fleet in Bremerton, Washington, where three years later she again briefly played the central role in ceremonies marking the fiftieth anniversary of the Japanese surrender. The navy had finally decided that the United States could no longer afford these great warships. By the Gulf War, the annual payroll alone of her all-volunteer crew was more than three times her total annual budget at the beginning of the Cold War in the late 1940s. In 1996, she was turned over to a private *Missouri* memorial foundation, and on June 22, 1998, she returned to Pearl Harbor for the last time. She is now permanently moored at Ford Island near the *Arizona* Memorial.

The Soviet withdrawal from Afghanistan and Eastern Europe, the decisive victory in the Gulf War, and the final collapse of the Soviet Union at the end of 1991 encouraged many to believe that the world was entering a new era of world peace and prosperity enforced by the American superpower. The U.S. Navy had a monopoly on great strategic warships able to demonstrate invincible American military force. The navy had perfected carrier warfare in the Pacific, building a fleet of *Essex*-class fleet carriers whose airplanes destroyed the Japanese navy. Although rendered obsolete by jet aircraft, many served not only in Korea but also in Vietnam.

The first real postwar generation of carriers, the four *Forrestal*-class ships, were twice as heavy and almost one hundred feet longer than the *Essex* class. Commissioned between 1955 and 1959, they served through the Cold War and Gulf War. One, *Ranger,* fought with *Missouri* and *Wisconsin* in the Persian Gulf. The last, *Independence,* was only decommissioned in September 1998 after *Harry S. Truman* joined the fleet. By the late 1950s it was clear that thanks to the strong-willed Admiral Hyman Rickover, nuclear energy would power the American submarine fleet. The value of nuclear power for surface ships was less clear however. The first nuclear-powered aircraft carrier, *Enterprise,* was the largest and most expensive warship ever built when she was commissioned in 1961. She was so

Harry S. Truman under construction at Norfolk.
(Defense Visual Information Center)

expensive, at $440 million, that Congress was reluctant to approve more nuclear carriers.

Only in 1967 did Congress finally authorize another nuclear aircraft carrier: *Nimitz*, CVN-68. This basic design proved so successful that in 1989 work began on the eighth *Nimitz*, *Harry S. Truman*, at Newport News Shipyard. These are the largest and most expensive warships ever built, costing over $4.5 billion each. They weigh over 70,000 tons, or over 100,000 tons fully loaded with crew, aircraft, aviation fuel, ammunition, and supplies. Their two Westinghouse reactors drive four General Electric steam turbines producing a total of 280,000 horsepower that propel them over 35 miles per hour. Their flight decks measure 1,096 feet by 251 feet, or over 4 acres, and carry 4 steam catapults to launch the 80 aircraft in their air wings. These are the first American warships to carry women as permanent crew members.

Because of their great size, *Harry S. Truman* and her sisters are built of 190 modules, some weighing as much as 900 tons. These giant building blocks are assembled in drydock using huge movable cranes. In all, 60,000 tons of steel and 900 miles of cable and wiring are used in construction. Once the hull is complete, the dock is flooded and the ship moved to a pier for completion. *Harry S. Truman*'s newest sister, *Ronald Reagan*, was completed in 2003. *Harry S. Truman* was christened on September 7, 1996. Sponsor Margaret Truman Daniel could not participate, but both Virginia senators and Missouri congressman Ike Skelton watched as a bottle of Missouri champagne was used to christen her. Two years later, on July 25, 1998, just one month after *Missouri* returned to Pearl Harbor for the last time, President Bill Clinton and Secretary of Defense William Cohen, along with Ike Skelton and Missouri governor Mel Carnahan, attended the commissioning. President Clinton said that the new nuclear carrier was an enduring way to remember the country's thirty-third president. Captain Thomas G. Otterbein responded: "The qualities of hard work, honesty, integrity, and moral courage which made Harry S Truman an enduring figure in our nation's history, also permeate this crew. I'm proud to be their captain."

The crew was equally proud of their ship. They designed an emblem combining eagles to symbolize Harry Truman's well-known integrity and honesty, the name Truman in the shape of the ship's hull, and his famous motto: "the buck stops here." The seal is embedded in the deck in many passageways, and a large seal is embedded on the bridge between the captain's chair and the ship's surprisingly small wooden wheel. The ship's battle flag also carries on the Truman tradition, being similar to the flag carried by Captain Harry Truman's World War I Battery D of the 129th

Field Artillery Regiment. Crossed artillery cannons are superimposed over carrier *Harry S. Truman*'s number, CVN-75, to symbolize the relationship between World War I firepower and the carrier's great power. As her executive officer, Captain Ted Carter, noted in October 2002, the ship carries by herself the seventh largest air force in the world. Finally, the flag carries the ship's battle cry: "Give 'em Hell." As crew members and visitors come aboard, they pass a small museum with one of Truman's World War I uniforms, his famous walking cane and fedora hat, and pictures and quotations from his life.

Longer than the Empire State Building, *Harry S. Truman* is literally a small floating city with some three thousand crew members and another two thousand men and women in her air wing. The ship has its own newspaper, television station, store, and hospital, as well as machine shops to keep herself and her aircraft operating. The crew keep track of news via satellite, and can communicate with their families via e-mail and videophone. Her kitchens serve over eighteen thousand meals a day, and one crewman told the *New York Times* that Captain Otterbein worked so hard to keep the crew happy that "this is a little slice of paradise." Several hundred women serve aboard, and although the ship is an enormously complicated and extremely hazardous floating airfield and high-tech war machine, over a thousand of her crew are high school graduates younger than twenty-one years old.

Harry S. Truman carries three fighter and fighter-attack squadrons as well as electronic warfare, early warning, and antisubmarine aircraft. No other nation on earth has ships like *Harry S. Truman* and her *Nimitz* sisters. Both during the Cold War and since, American aircraft carriers have been stationed around the world in critical areas, especially the Mediterranean, western Pacific, and Indian Ocean and Persian Gulf. Each ship remains on station for six months and then is replaced by another carrier while it returns to its home port for overhaul and training. The *Nimitz* sisters are designed for fifty years of active service and only require refueling every twenty-five years or every million miles of steaming. They carry more than three million gallons of jet fuel for their aircraft but can be resupplied at sea during their six-month tours.

Harry S. Truman has 2 squadrons of McDonnell Douglas F/A-18 fighter-bombers, the "Bulls" and the "Gunslingers." These planes, built in St. Louis, Missouri, weigh 66,000 pounds, have a top speed of 1,180 miles per hour, and can carry deadly smart bombs able to hit small targets with pinpoint accuracy.

Powerful as she is, *Harry S. Truman* is only the center-piece of a huge battle group, which also includes a cruiser, five destroyers, a frigate, a nuclear attack submarine, and two supply ships. With fifteen thousand sailors, the battle group protects and resupplies *Harry S. Truman* while she remains ready at any time day or night to send her aircraft against America's enemies.

From her Norfolk base, *Harry S. Truman*'s crew and pilots spent 1999 and 2000 training and preparing for their first six-month operational cruise. Because the navy was finding it difficult to recruit enough sailors for its world-wide commitments, *Harry S. Truman* went to sea lacking several hundred crew members. Her crew thus had to work longer shifts, often twelve hours at a time, and many sailors had to take on additional duties to keep the ship operating. Just before her first full deployment, her sailors received a painful reminder from another Missouri ship of the new threats facing America and the navy.

During the Cold War, the greatest threat to American national interests and the U.S. Navy came from the Soviet Union and other rival states. As the Soviet threat disap-peared, Americans found themselves under increasing attack all over the world from shadowy terrorist groups. While no country can challenge the American fleet, small groups of suicidal terrorists could strike as the navy is called upon to carry out American foreign policy in the world's most dangerous regions.

Cole is one of the first 28 original *Arleigh Burke*-class guided missile destroyers designed to defend aircraft carriers against attack by aircraft or missiles. These ships are equipped with Aegis antiaircraft defense systems so sophisticated that they can even be used in the new national missile defense against ballistic missile attack. Weighing 6,000 tons, and powered by four General Electric turbines with a total of 100,000 horsepower, *Cole* carries a crew of 22 officers and 315 sailors. She is very heavily armed, with 90 Tomahawks, antisubmarine torpedoes, one 5-inch gun, and two Phalanx antimissile guns. She cost almost $1 billion and was built by Litton/Ingalls Shipyard in Pascagoula, Mississippi. At 505 feet, the *Arleigh Burkes* are almost as big as the World War II cruiser *St. Louis,* and unlike many modern lightweight warships, they are built of high-strength steel with extra Kevlar armor. *Cole,* the seventeenth *Arleigh Burke,* was launched in February 1995 and commissioned in June of 1996. She was named for marine sergeant Darrell Samuel Cole, born on July 20, 1920, in Flat River, Missouri. He enlisted in the marines on August 25, 1941, "for the duration of the national emergency" and was assigned as a battlefield messenger. He was sent to Guadalcanal during the bitter jungle fighting and proved himself as a machine gunner. He fought in some of the bloodiest island campaigns of the Pacific war, was wounded, and earned the Purple Heart and Bronze Star for his "resolute leadership, indomitable fighting spirit, and tenacious determination in the face of terrific opposition." On February 19, 1945, Sergeant Cole led his machine gun team ashore during the first assault on Iwo Jima. Under heavy fire, he personally destroyed several Japanese bunkers with hand grenades before being killed by an enemy grenade. He received the Medal of Honor for

Sergeant Darrell Cole.
(U.S. Marine Corps,
Medal of Honor file)

his: "dauntless initiative, unfaltering courage, indomitable determination. . . . Sergeant Cole served as an inspiration to his comrades, and his stouthearted leadership in the face of almost certain death sustained and enhanced the highest traditions of the U.S. Naval Service. He gallantly gave his life for his country."

Cole left her homeport, Norfolk, August 8, 2000, on her way to the Persian Gulf. Among her crew was Chief Gunner's Mate Norm Larson, who had been with *Cole* since her commissioning four years earlier and was in charge of her powerful missile battery. His mother lives in Columbia, Missouri, and his sister on a nearby farm. In October, *Cole* stopped for fuel at the port of Aden in Yemen. Her captain, Commander Kirk S. Lippold, had been an aide to the secretary of the navy and was known as an outstanding officer, a careful, precise "water walker" destined for great success. Still, he considered Aden to be so safe that his guards carried unloaded weapons as they watched small boats unloading garbage and bringing food and supplies to the ship. Just before noon on October 12, 2000, as many of *Cole*'s crew were lined up in her mess hall, two Arabs in another small motorboat approached the ship and waved at the watching guards. They waved back as the two men stood at attention and detonated several hundred pounds of high explosives. The blast tore a hole forty square feet in the ship just at the mess hall and engine room, killing seventeen crew members and wounding forty-two others. As a female sailor wrote to her family:

> The ship list[ed] to the port side. I have never seen such a horrible sight. Everything was blown toward the starboard side and mangled. There were people pinned against the walls, body parts in and under metal . . . very few people cried. How we avoided [a fire] is a mystery to everyone.

As a thousand tons of water poured into *Cole*, her crew rallied to stop the flooding, restore light and power, and help the wounded. Chief Larson, who was only seventy-five feet from the explosion, was thrown violently against the door of his office. Although he first thought *Cole* had been rammed by another ship or had suffered an accidental fuel explosion, he ordered other sailors to their battle stations and got a rifle from the armory. Larson then escorted Captain Lippold to the bridge and organized security guards to protect the crippled ship.

With no toilets or showers the crew worked around the clock for five days in terrible heat until the last bodies were recovered from the flooded engine room. Within a day, FBI investigators arrived, and within a month U.S. and Yemeni authorities blamed the attack on Usama bin Laden's al Qaeda organization, which two years earlier had killed 224 and wounded 6,000 with bombs at the American embassies in Dar es Salaam, Tanzania, and Nairobi, Kenya. Following the destruction of the World Trade Towers in 2001, the U.S.

Cole departing from Yemen.
(Defense Visual Information Center)

Cole on *Blue Marlin*
(Defense Visual Information Center)

launched a worldwide counterattack on al Qaeda. Two years after the attack on *Cole*, the suspected ringleader of the attack, Abu Ali al-Harithi, was killed by a missile fired by an American Predator unmanned aerial vehicle in the Yemeni desert. Another ringleader was captured and is in custody.

An American admiral, who had commanded *Cole's* original sister *Arleigh Burke*, praised Lippold and his crew:

> That captain obviously trained his crew to survive and thrive in the chaos . . . at the very instant the bomb exploded. There is no higher praise for a captain.
>
> That well-trained crew, *Cole's* men and women, obviously saved their ship despite losing some of their shipmates. There is no tougher fight, and there is no tougher crew than one that saves a ship.
>
> Last but not least, we should not forget the brilliant American designers, engineers, and shipbuilders who built . . . "505 feet of American fighting steel."

Two hundred of her crew stayed with *Cole* until the end of October, when she was towed out of Aden harbor flying a huge American flag and playing "The Star-Spangled Banner," "America the Beautiful," and Kid Rock's popular "Cowboy." As the American ambassador said: "*[Cole]* left with some help from her friends, but she left proudly." After *Cole* was loaded aboard the huge Norwegian ship *Blue Marlin* for the long trip back to the Ingalls shipyard in Pascagoula, the crew that had remained with *Cole* flew home together back to their waiting families in Norfolk. As Captain Lippold said, they "return[ed] home as one crew, forever bonded by this experience."

Following a thorough investigation, Admiral Vern Clark, chief of naval operations, sent a message to the fleet:

> This is the first successful terrorist attack against a navy ship in modern times . . . the world is full of risk and there

are those who are determined to bring harm to America and America's navy. . . . The actions of *Cole*'s crew immediately following the blast are highly commendable. Undoubtedly through their discipline, training, and courage they saved their ship and many of their shipmates. Without the efforts of every member of USS *Cole*, this tragedy could have been much worse. Under the harshest of conditions, they persevered through devastation and horror that many of us have never seen. They saved their ship and the lives of many of their shipmates. Their service is a wonderful example to us all.

Cole arrived back in Pascagoula in December 2000. Chief Larson, who remembered many of the shipyard workers from 1995 when the ship was being built, stayed with *Cole* offering advice on reconstruction for several months until he was given another assignment. On April 19, 2002, hundreds cheered as she sailed out of Pascagoula after a repair that cost $250 million and included new engines and other upgrades. At the end of April she was back in Norfolk, although only forty sailors who had been aboard in Aden were still in her crew. *Cole* now has a "hall of heroes" with seventeen stars embedded in the passageway, and as the father of nineteen-year-old crew member Lakeina Monique Francis said of his dead child: "My daughter is part of the ship."

A month after the wounded *Cole* was towed out of Aden harbor to begin the long voyage home, families gathered in Norfolk to watch *Harry S. Truman* and her battle group depart for a six-month deployment to the Mediterranean and the Persian Gulf. Sad that their sailors and marines would be away from home at Christmas, they also worried for the safety of their loved ones. As one wife said: "I know this is the mother ship and she's very protected . . . but its hard not to be concerned, especially with current events." The battle group commander, Rear Admiral James D. MacArthur Jr. tried to reassure the families: "our sailors

Harry S. Truman leaving on first deployment. (Defense Visual Information Center)

and marines have worked hard and trained harder over many months. . . . Our people understand the importance of our mission and are prepared to meet any challenges we may face."

Harry S. Truman left Norfolk on November 28, 2000, but on their way to the Middle East the crew received an early Christmas present when they were visited by astronaut John Glenn, Secretary of Defense William Cohen, and a group of football stars and entertainers who broadcast Fox TV's "NFL Live" football show from the flight deck. Star quarterback Terry Bradshaw was even taught to steer the carrier, and the Dallas cheerleaders and the pop singer Jewel performed for the crew in front of a huge portrait of Truman on the hangar deck.

As soon as *Harry S. Truman* reached the Persian Gulf, her pilots joined the patrols enforcing the "no-fly" zone in southern Iraq, and her small escort warships helped prevent smugglers from violating United Nations economic sanctions against Iraq. Ever since the end of the Gulf War in 1991, Saddam Hussein had been threatening allied pilots. On February 16, 2001, in the heaviest air attacks in two years, *Harry S. Truman* aircraft attacked Iraqi air defense radars and command and control centers near Baghdad. The pilots used 1,500 pound satellite-guided "Joint Stand-off Weapons," which cost as much as $750,000 each and can be dropped as far as 40 miles from their targets. To their disappointment, as many as half of these very sophisticated and expensive bombs missed their targets. The navy decided that the computers in the bombs had been improperly programmed, but the unexpectedly poor performance of these costly weapons led to sharp criticism in American newspapers. Just a month later, another *Harry S. Truman* pilot was involved in a tragic accident in Kuwait. On March 12, an F/A-18 Hornet pilot was practicing close air support to ground forces. His bomb fell short of his target, killing five Americans and a New Zealander and wounding five other soldiers. During a speech at the time, President George W. Bush called for a moment of silence and noted: "I'm reminded today of how dangerous service can be."

By the summer of 2001, *Harry S. Truman* and her battle group were back in Norfolk, but the pace of training continued. Each time the carrier returns her pilots fly their aircraft to nearby naval air stations where the airplanes are inspected, maintained, and repaired, and where the pilots spend their shore time perfecting their skills. The carrier herself is restocked for her next deployment, and new crew members are trained and integrated into the *Harry S. Truman* team. During their time in Norfolk the battle group makes brief training cruises into the Atlantic and Caribbean. During one such cruise during the summer of 2002, former president George H. W. Bush came aboard for an overnight visit. Watching night landings and takeoffs, the most dangerous activities on any carrier, the former World War II carrier pilot said: "What I saw on the flight deck was teamwork. . . . It was unbelievable. The ship has a soul . . . a spirit." In December 2002 *Harry S. Truman* again left Norfolk, headed for another war against Iraq.

For over one hundred and seventy-five years, the soul and spirit described by President Bush has motivated the American sailors serving in Missouri ships. Whether protecting American diplomatic and economic interests, or fighting the nation's enemies, the ships have carried the Show-Me spirit and the American flag around the world. The first *St. Louis* confronted a great European empire, the second helped save the Union itself, and a later *St. Louis* fought from the first day of World War II until the very end. The war ended on the deck of the "Mighty Mo," and the last battleship in history fought in the last world war, the first war of the Cold War, and the first war of the post-Cold War world. The three latest Missouri ships, *Jefferson City*, *Cole*, and *Harry S. Truman*, face new threats and new enemies in a new century in which danger no longer comes from rival great power navies. Despite their great power, these new ships must exercise this power with unprecedented precision. *Jefferson City* can carry special operations SEAL teams who use stealth to reach their targets. Both *Jefferson City* and *Cole* can use their Tomahawk guided missiles against small targets hundreds of miles away—whether they are terrorist camps, radar sites, or weapons factories. And *Harry S. Truman* can bring the overwhelming power of her air wing to bear against terrorists or hostile countries almost anywhere on earth. All three ships should continue to serve for decades, reminding new generations of sailors of Missouri's contributions to American naval history.

For More Reading

BOOKS

At War at Sea, by Ronald H. Spector (New York: Viking Press, 2001), covers high points of twentieth-century naval history.

Eagle against the Sun, by Ronald H. Spector (New York: Vintage Books, 1985), focuses exclusively on the war in the Pacific against Japan.

A History of the Confederate Navy, by Raimondo Luraghi (Annapolis: Naval Institute Press, 1996), and *By River and By Sea: The Naval History of the Civil War,* by Bern Anderson (New York: Da Capo Press, 1989), are two solid histories, although Anderson's book was originally published in 1962 and Luraghi's is translated from the original Italian.

The Fifty Year War, by Norman Friedman (Annapolis: Naval Institute Press, 2000), is a detailed discussion of Cold War history, concentrating on military issues and technology.

Theodore Roosevelt and the Great White Fleet: American Sea Power Comes of Age, by Kenneth Wimmel (Dulles, Virginia: Brassey's, 2000), is a general history of the great naval race leading to the First World War, describing how the United States decided to become a naval power.

This People's Navy: The Making of American Sea Power, by Kenneth J. Hagan (New York: Free Press, 1991), traces the history of the American navy through the end of the Cold War.

The Two-Ocean War: A Short History of the United States Navy in the Second World War, by Samuel Eliot Morrison (New York: Galahad Books, 1997), is this distinguished naval historian's "brief" distillation of his authoritative multivolume history of the war.

ONLINE RESOURCES

Many wonderful pictures are available online at a variety of government and unofficial websites. The following are among the most interesting sources of naval images.

The Defense Visual Information Center website, www.dodmedia.osd.mil. This site contains current images of all the American military services.

An unofficial site, www.hazegray.org, includes a variety of images of American and foreign warships.

The U.S. Naval Historical Center website, www.history.navy.mil, includes a large collection of historical images and information on American naval history.

The official U.S. Navy website, www.navy.mil, offers interesting links to such modern ships as *Cole* and *Harry S. Truman.*

Index

About the Author

Photo by Leah W. Schroeder

Richard E. Schroeder holds a Ph.D. in modern military history from the University of Chicago. He retired from the Central Intelligence Agency's Clandestine Service after a three-decade career spent in Europe and Washington, D.C. He held the CIA chair at National Defense University's Industrial College of the Armed Forces, is an adjunct professor in Georgetown University's Security Studies Program, and is a member of the board of advisors of the International Spy Museum in Washington, D.C. He lives with his wife, Leah, in Arlington, Virginia.